The Charms of Miss O'Hara

Tales of *Gone With the Wind*
& the Golden Age of Hollywood
from Scarlett's Little Sister

PHILLIP DONE

GATEWAY PUBLISHING
Mountain View, CA 94040

Cover Design: Brian Halley
Cover Photograph: Connie Sutherland
Author Photo: Paul Corfield
Interior Design: Polgarus Studio

Manufactured in the United States of America

ISBN-13: 978-0-6159-8731-6
ISBN-10: 0-6159-8731-1

Dedicated to:

The Marietta Gone With the Wind Museum

ALSO BY PHILLIP DONE

32 Third Graders and One Class Bunny:
Life Lessons from Teaching

Close Encounters of the Third-Grade Kind:
Thoughts on Teacherhood

Praise for *The Charms of Miss O'Hara*

"A joyous book about a joyous person. Rich with tenderness, warmth, and wit, *The Charms of Miss O'Hara* is a touching tribute to a dear friend whose company I always enjoyed. Now, in these pages, you get to enjoy her company, too."

— Debbie Reynolds, star of *Singin' in the Rain* and author of the *New York Times* bestseller *Unsinkable*

"Ann Rutherford, Scarlett O'Hara's younger sister and Andy Hardy's perky girlfriend, Polly Benedict, was a more memorable person off-screen than on, and Phillip Done has caught her inimitable voice, her charm, her humanity and her humor in this book of their late, but rewarding friendship for them and for Mr. Done's readers."

— Anne Edwards, author of *Vivien Leigh: A Biography* and *Road to Tara: The Life of Margaret Mitchell*

"Although Ann Rutherford passed away in 2012, Phillip Done's magical memoir of Hollywood's ultimate sweet young sister/girl next-door gives readers a chance to meet this delightful woman up close and personal. Done perfectly captures the many charms of Miss Rutherford, especially her wonderful sense of humor and her great love for her fans. And reading Ann's memories of the Golden Age of Hollywood is like strolling hand-in-hand with Polly Benedict to the malt shop — down memory lane to a time that, sadly, is now gone with the wind."

— John Wiley Jr., editor of *The Scarlett Letters: The Making of the Film* Gone With the Wind

"A splendid book ... Annie would have been so pleased. She was my delightful friend ... I miss her."

— Anne Jeffreys, star of stage, screen, and the television series *Topper*

"A rare, amazing opportunity to meet and know a classic, classy Hollywood star. You'll come away feeling you were right there at Rutherford's side, sharing every enthralling memory, clear-eyed observation, and humorous aside. She remains a treasure; the book is her equal."

— John Fricke, author of *Judy: A Legendary Film Career* and *The Wonderful World of Oz.*

"What a wonderful tribute to Ann Rutherford! Phil Done is to be commended for exploring a yet unexplored Hollywood niche — the life of one of Hollywood's most beautiful ladies and her connections to — and stories about — many of the industry's most revered films. Every *Gone With the Wind* fan should read this book."

— Michael Troyan, author of *MGM: Hollywood's Greatest Backlot* and *Greer Garson: The Rose of Mrs. Miniver*

"Phil Done has discovered Ann Rutherford's voice, telling her story in Ann's own indomitable way. Ann would have been so proud."

— Christopher P. Sullivan, M.D., owner of the Marietta Gone With the Wind Museum collection

"Since June 2012, the special place in my heart for my friend Ann Rutherford has been empty. But, no less than a miracle occurred during my reading of Phillip Done's book *The Charms of Miss O'Hara,* a first-hand account of his time with Ann. The emptiness disappeared and wonderful memories replaced it. Thank you, Phillip, for this incredible tribute to the first lady of Greenway Drive. It truly 'happied' me."

— Connie Sutherland, director of the Marietta Gone With the Wind Museum

Do not squander time. That is the stuff life is made of.

— *Gone With the Wind*, sign at Twelve Oaks

Ann Rutherford wears her beloved locket.
— photo courtesy of the Patrick Picking Collection

Introduction

When Peter Pan stands outside the nursery window and peeks in at Wendy, Michael, and John, he comes for one reason only — to hear the stories. It always saddens me that when someone leaves this world, too often their stories go with them. Not long ago, actress Ann Rutherford, best known as Scarlett's youngest sister in *Gone With the Wind*, passed from this earth. She and I met near the end of her long, rich life. Our meeting was not by chance. I know that now. Thankfully, her stories remain. I couldn't let them go. Within these pages, Miss Rutherford's words are hers. Some of our conversations were recorded. Others I wrote down so that I wouldn't forget. Their details seem to have etched themselves in my mind — like scenes from a beautiful film that stays with you long after it is over. This book is a tribute to an incredible woman, a love letter to a friend. May Miss Rutherford's voice and spirit touch your heart as they did mine — and may her memory forever ride the wind.

The Movie Star

Live! Life is a banquet, and most poor suckers are
starving to death.

— *Auntie Mame*

It was a warm summer evening in 2005. My editor, Heidi, and I were drinking our second round of Kir Royales at the Cinegrill Lounge in Hollywood's Roosevelt Hotel while waiting for the concert to begin. Michael Feinstein would be performing that night. We had driven down from Northern California to celebrate the release of my first book. The room, with its potted palms, tufted booths, and miniature deco lamps on each round table reminded me of one of those sleek clubs you'd see in a Fred Astaire-Ginger Rogers picture.

"You know," Heidi said, "they say that this old hotel is haunted."

"*Really?*" I said, intrigued.

"Yes."

I changed my voice to sound like Vincent Price. "Then maybe we'll meet some old Hollywood ghosts clanking around tonight."

Just then I noticed a tall man standing a few feet away. He was speaking to an elderly woman seated at the next table. Her back was to Heidi. The man was clearly excited. Eavesdropping, I heard him say a word that caused my eyebrows to shoot up: *Atlanta.*

Immediately my mind started racing: one exuberant man … here in Hollywood … an older woman … Atlanta … *Could it be?* Raising my chin, I peered over Heidi's shoulder to get a better look at the woman. She was elegantly dressed in gray chiffon. Her hair — the color of my champagne. A handsome, white-haired gentleman wearing a red, polka-dotted ascot and a matching pocket square sat across from her. As I observed the scene, the man who stood handed the woman a paper cocktail napkin and asked her to autograph it.

I leaned in to Heidi and dropped my voice to a whisper. "Don't look. I think the woman behind you is a movie star." Heidi started to turn. "Don't turn around."

"Why do you think that?" Heidi whispered back.

"Because the man standing behind you just asked for her autograph. And he said *Atlanta.*"

Heidi screwed up her face. "I don't get it."

"Atlanta was where *Gone With the Wind* premiered," I said. "*That* woman was in *Gone With the Wind.* I know it."

"Aren't all the cast members dead?"

"No," I said, scooting back my chair. "A couple of them are still alive."

"Where are you going?"

"To find out who it is."

As I stood up, Heidi grabbed my arm and gave me a grin. "Maybe she's a ghost."

"Very funny."

I hurried to the entrance of the lounge and found the hostess. "Excuse me," I said, "there's a woman sitting next to my table." I pointed toward my seat. "See. Over there. She's with an older gentleman. Can you tell me who that is?"

The hostess glanced across the room. "Yes," she said. "That's Ann

Rutherford."

It felt like firecrackers started going off in my chest. "Ann *Rutherford?*" I said, stepping back.

A former MGM contractee, Ann Rutherford played Polly Benedict, Mickey Rooney's girlfriend, in the Andy Hardy pictures, performed with Laurence Olivier and Greer Garson in *Pride and Prejudice*, and was Scarlett's youngest sister, Carreen, in *Gone With the Wind*. I looked back at where she was sitting. I *had* to meet her. Quickly I walked over, tucking my shirt in on the way. When I reached her table, Miss Rutherford looked up at me with a warm smile.

"Uh … excuse me," I said. My voice had risen. "I'm … I'm so sorry to bother you, but the hostess just told me that you're Ann Rutherford." I clasped my hands together. "It's such a pleasure to meet you, Miss Rutherford. My name is Phillip Done. I'm a huge fan."

"Well, thank you, Phillip." Her voice was warm, too.

Miss Rutherford introduced me to her friend, whose name was Al Morley. He half-stood and gave me a strong handshake. Then I turned back and excitedly started rattling off the names of as many of her films as I could remember: *Orchestra Wives, Adventures of Don Juan, Whistling in Dixie, The Secret Life of Walter Mitty*. I purposely didn't mention *Gone With the Wind* because I wanted her to know I was a *true* fan.

"Honey," she said, merrily, "you have made my day."

Then Miss Rutherford did something that absolutely floored me. She asked Al if he would switch seats with me until the concert started. Grinning, Al took it in stride. It seemed as though it wasn't the first time he'd been asked to give up his seat for a fan. As Al stood, I stepped over to Heidi, who had been listening to the conversation. "Heidi, meet Al. Al — Heidi." I returned to Miss Rutherford, who motioned for me to take a seat. Then I sat down with a movie star.

"Is that Phillip with one *l* or two?" she asked, smiling.

"Two."

She reached out her hand and shook mine. "Nice to meet you, Phillip with two *l*s."

The light from the table lamp shone on her face like a footlight, illuminating her big brown eyes. For her age — she had to be in her eighties — she was still striking. I couldn't contain my excitement. "You look ... beautiful!"

Her laugh had music in it, like crystal touched in a toast. "Well, aren't you sweet." Then she leaned in and lowered her voice. "Honey, if you haven't noticed, I'm the only woman in this town who doesn't color her hair. All my girlfriends are either blondes or redheads, but I'm just too lazy to wrap my hair up in Reynolds Wrap."

We laughed together.

Though I tried to keep the conversation on her, Miss Rutherford wanted to know all about me. I told her that I was a grade-school teacher in California and that I had just written my first book about my life in the classroom. I explained that I was in Beverly Hills to celebrate its release. Miss Rutherford was genuinely thrilled. She laughed when I said that sitting with her was more exciting than visiting with the Queen of England. I wasn't kidding. Had I been given a choice between the queen and Ann Rutherford, the queen would be sitting with Al.

No question about it — I was crazy about old Hollywood. The bookshelves in my home were filled with biographies of classic movie stars. The walls were decorated with posters from famous films:

Gaslight, It's a Wonderful Life, An American in Paris, Meet Me in St. Louis. My DVDs — all Turner classics. If anyone asked me if there was another time and place that I wished I'd lived, I wouldn't have to even think about it: the 1930s and '40s. Hollywood. I was a throwback, for sure. In my fantasy world, I would have worked at MGM polishing Fred Astaire's shoes, carrying Lana Turner's makeup case, fetching Clark Gable's coffee, and refilling the Wicked Witch's bucket of water between takes of *The Wizard of Oz.* Anything!

Even as a kid I was in love with old movies. I remember in fourth grade my teacher asked the class to give oral reports on famous people we admired. We could dress up like the person if we wanted to. While everyone else was speaking about David Cassidy and Donnie Osmond, I came in dressed as the Tin Man with a funnel on my head. That same year, after seeing *Singin' in the Rain* on television, I ran and jumped around the house performing "Make 'Em Laugh" like Donald O'Connor. My mom didn't appreciate the shoe prints on the walls. Around the same time, I walked inside one day, soaking wet. I'd been hanging on a street lamp and splashing in puddles with an umbrella like Gene Kelly.

I leaned in to Miss Rutherford with a smile that could not have been any bigger. "What was it like to be a movie star in the golden age of Hollywood?"

"Honey," she said, slapping her hands on the table, "it was absolutely glorious."

"Did you know you were living in the golden era?"

"I had no idea. None of us did. When we were cranking out those movies, working day and night on those dark soundstages, it never occurred to us. We were too focused on the next take. Had I known I was living in the golden age, I would have tried to enjoy it more." Then her lips curled into a smile. "Actually, I don't think I could have."

"Miss Rutherford ..."

"Call me Ann."

I felt goose bumps.

"Ann." It seemed strange saying that. "How did you get started in show business?"

"Well, the books will tell you that I performed as a young child, but that's all baloney. I did plays as a kid, but just school plays like everyone else. I was Raggedy Ann in one and Humpty Dumpty in another. When I started in pictures, the studio had to give me a background, so the publicists made all that up. I always loved an audience though. I remember when I was in grade school, standing on stage in the spelling bee. My word was *honey*. I loudly proclaimed, '*Honey*. H-U-N-Y.' The audience started laughing. I loved it and told myself, 'I have to do that again.' Laughter was always like liquor to me." *

We both chuckled.

"How did you break into pictures?" I asked.

"I was in radio first," she said.

"I didn't know that. Then how did you get into radio?"

"I lied."

I let out a laugh. And then, like a child riveted by a favorite storybook, I listened closely as Ann remembered.

---

* According to a February 20, 1941, article in *The Evening Times*, Ann's first theatrical job was in a San Francisco stock company's production of *Mrs. Wiggs of the Cabbage Patch* when she was in the first grade. None of this, Ann said, was true.

Radio

I *literally rolled into my career. It was the early 1930s. I was 15. After school, I used to roller skate home with my girlfriends past the KFAC radio station in Los Angeles. The building stood on Wilshire Boulevard opposite the Cocoanut Grove and the Ambassador Hotel. On the ground floor, they had a showroom for Cord automobiles, and my friends and I would press our noses against the windows to look at the fancy cars. Once in a while, if we didn't have a lot of homework, we would take our skates off, hide them in the bushes, and ride the elevator up to the station to watch the show. We sat in what was called the "viewing" room — it sounds like Forest Lawn — a glass booth with a couple of sofas and overstuffed chairs. The performers stood behind a window. I loved the sound effects man, who'd rattle a metal thing to make thunder, or drop a sack of sugar on the floor to sound like someone fell over, or clomp two half-coconut shells like galloping horses.*

As we watched the show, I'd observe the performers closely. One day, one of them walked near the glass, and I could see his script. The pages were marked with pencil; these were obviously his lines. I was fascinated by the caution with which the actors stood in front of the microphone, not too close, not too far away. Just right. And if they weren't dropping their papers to the floor when they finished reading a page, which looked so untidy if there was an audience, they would reach their arms way out in front so that the paper turning wouldn't be picked up in the microphone.

Well, one day my history teacher — Miss Farrell was her name — kept me after school. I had just discovered the writer Edna St. Vincent Millay. I just fell over reading anything she wrote. I should have been reading about the Ancient Phoenicians, but instead I was deep in thought, composing a poem. I, too, wanted to be a poetess. As I scribbled on my paper, that slippery teacher came slithering behind me and whisked the page out from under my pencil. Then she called everyone to attention and proceeded to read it to the class, ever so poorly. She put the emphasis on all the wrong syllables. It was a real mess. When she finished, Miss Farrell looked down at me and announced that I could assist her for a good half hour after school and see that the blackboards were immaculate. Needless to say, I was not happy.

The second I finished cleaning those boards, I roller skated as quickly as I could out of there. As I approached KFAC, I thought — boy, if I had a job I wouldn't have to go to that crummy school anymore. So, I stopped, unstrapped my skates, parked them behind a potted palm, and rode the elevator up to the station. When I got upstairs, I asked the receptionist where I go to apply for a job. "For what?" she asked. "I'm an actress," I said. I'd never acted in my life. She didn't think it was crazy to see a fifteen-year-old kid with schoolbooks under her arm because back then they used kids in radio. It was very difficult for an adult to sound like a child. The woman pointed me to the casting director down the hall, and I stepped into his office and explained why I was there. When he asked me about my experience, I started rattling off a long list of shows, none of which I'd been in.

Back then, there used to be a repertory company called the Henry Duffy Players, which rotated between San Francisco and Los Angeles. Every Saturday, if there was nothing good playing at the Orpheum like Sophie Tucker or The Duncan Sisters, my mother would take my sister

Judith and me downtown on the streetcar to see a play. In the thirties, you could ride the streetcar from Wilshire and Fairfax all the way downtown for seven cents. I remember my sister and I would wear gloves. In my day, young ladies always wore gloves when going to the theater. We'd save all the programs and talk about the performances and the actors. So, when that casting director asked me what shows I'd been in, I just named every single play I remembered seeing that had a kid in it. I lied like a rug. I must have named everything except Dinner at Eight. *The man seemed pretty impressed. He took my name and phone number. When I got home, I didn't tell my mother or my grandmother what I'd done.*

About a month later, I came home from school, and my mother was waiting for me at the top of the stairs with her arms crossed. Not a good sign.

"Ann, have you been making a nuisance of yourself down at KFAC?" she asked in a tone that sounded like she'd already made up her mind.

"No," I replied. "Why?"

"The station just called. They want you down there right away."

"Oh, boy!" I said. "That's good."

I put my skates back on and whizzed down to KFAC. When I arrived, there were two lines of kids, one for girls and another for boys. They were all about my age. A man came along and gave everyone three pages. The girls were reading for the part of Nancy, and the boys for the role of Dick. We were auditioning for a Saturday serial called Nancy and Dick: The Spirit of '76. *It was sponsored by the Daughters of the American Revolution and the Broadway Department Store.*

The first thing I did was take the pencil from behind my ear — I always stuck a pencil in my hair — and made bold lines under everything that said Nancy. I didn't have a book to write on, so I borrowed the back of the girl in front of me. When it came time to read my lines, I was very cautious about how far away I stood from the microphone. Back then they were as big as dessert plates. I couldn't wait to turn a page. When it was time to do so, I reached out like a giraffe and turned the paper as quietly as I could so it wouldn't sound like a forest fire in the microphone. Well, wouldn't you know it — I got the part of Nancy! I'd be paid five dollars a week. This was the height of the Depression. Nobody had a real job then. Men were selling apples on the streets. By George, here I was fifteen years old, and I got a real job!

Backstage

If you obey all the rules, you miss all the fun.

— Katharine Hepburn

Ann laughed. "So here I got the job, and I *still* had to go to that crummy school."

"Did you do other radio shows?" I asked.

"Oh, yes," Ann answered. "One show led to another. I did another show called *Calling All Cars*. Later, I did *The Eddie Bracken Show* for a couple of years. Then in the '40s, I replaced Penny Singleton as Blondie. It was all live back then — nothing was taped. We would go in on Wednesdays, rehearse a little, and return on Thursdays. We performed one show for the East Coast, ate dinner at the Brown Derby, then came back and did a second show for the California coast. That was it." Ann grinned. "It was very easy work, the closest thing to stealing money I ever experienced."

The station insisted that Ann wear a blonde wig for the show. "Why do I have to wear a wig?" she asked. "It's radio, for goodness' sake. I can't be seen." They said that the studio audience could see her, and that every time her husband called Blondie they'd laugh because she didn't have blonde hair. So, Ann went to Max Factor and bought herself a blonde wig.

As Ann and I talked, a couple of musicians came out on stage and started warming up. I noticed Al push back his seat.

"It looks like the concert is about to start," I said, standing up. "Thank you so much for letting me sit with you like this." Ann extended her hand, and I nearly kissed it.

When I returned to my table, Heidi leaned in. "Well?" she whispered eagerly. All I could do was spin my head around like Wile E. Coyote after the Road Runner drops an anvil on his head.

During the concert, it was hard for me to focus on the music. I kept stealing glances at Ann. A couple of times Al caught me looking at her, and I'd throw him a smile. At the intermission, I wanted to go over and visit some more, but I refrained. I didn't want to overdo it. When the concert was over, I stepped over to Ann and asked if she'd sign my cocktail napkin, too. She did so happily and signed her name with a flourish — just like a movie star's ought to be.

The four of us stepped out of the lounge together and said our good-byes in the hotel lobby. Ann and Al didn't walk toward the front door, but proceeded down a hall on the side of the club.

"I'll bet they're going backstage," I said to Heidi. "Want to join them?"

"They won't let you backstage," Heidi said.

"Sure they will." I grabbed her arm. "Follow me."

When we reached the stage door, a big burly guy with a badge and a clipboard stood guard. I said we were with Ann Rutherford and pointed to Ann's name on his list. He waved us in. After we walked through the double doors, I flashed Heidi a giant grin. "See."

The hallway was full of people. Ann spotted Heidi and me and welcomed us into her little circle. "Phil's a teacher," Ann said proudly. "And he just wrote a book." I was touched. She didn't know me from Adam and here she was bragging about me like I was her favorite grandson.

Ann "Blondie" Rutherford and Arthur "Dagwood" Lake bone up on their
French for an ABC radio broadcast of *Blondie* (1949).
— photo courtesy of the James Bawden Collection

A few minutes later, Ann was pulled away, and Heidi and I remained with Al. He and Ann had met twenty years earlier in Hollywood and were now best friends. He was Ann's travel companion. She never went on a big trip without him. "They call me Driving Miss Daisy," Al joked. "She takes me along because I'm good at spotting her luggage on the carousels." Al smiled. "I make sure Ann gets where she needs to be. On our last trip, we were on our way to an autograph signing, and I was waiting for her in the hotel lobby. There was no sign of her, so I went upstairs and knocked on the door. It was unlocked. And there she was sitting on the bed with her arm in a box of Cheerios. They were all over the bed. 'These are really good!' she said. 'I really like these.' Ann took them along to the signing."

As Heidi and I laughed, Al looked over at Ann with a broad smile. She was talking with friends. Then he turned back. "She's one of a kind," he said. "We laugh together constantly. I've never known anyone who enjoys life more than she does, and she lives it to the hilt. Her motto is: Miss Nothing. And she misses *nothing*. Did you know that she turned down the part of the older Rose in *Titanic*?"

"Why?" Heidi and I asked at the same time.

Just then Ann joined our huddle.

"I was just explaining that you turned down the part of Rose," Al said.

"Yes," Ann said. "I think they rounded up all the old gals in Hollywood for that part. They tried to entice me by saying they were going to shoot in places like Mexico. I said, 'Are you *crazy?* I've been on location shoots in Mexico before, and everyone ends up getting sick.' They also said they would shoot in Poland. '*Poland?*' I said, 'On *purpose?* '" Ann shook her head. "I didn't want to go to Poland."

"But think of all the fan mail you'd have gotten," Heidi said.

"I can't handle the fan mail I get now," Ann replied.

"Would you like to do another movie?" I asked.

"No!" Ann cried. "That's work!"

The four of us started talking about Ann's first films. Ann began her film career at Mascot Pictures, which soon became Republic. The studio made a lot of westerns, or "horse operas" as they were sometimes referred to, and Ann loved making them. They often shot on location in places like Lone Pine, Victorville, and Chatsworth. On the first day of her first western, Ann recalled watching the cowboys ride across the hill with their leather flying and making all sorts of racket. They did this until lunchtime. After lunch, the cowboys vanished. When they returned, they were all Indians in dark makeup. "Then," Ann began giggling, "they spent the rest of the day chasing themselves."

"John Wayne got his start at Mascot," Al joined in. "And Ann was his first leading lady."

"Y-*ep*," Ann answered with a twang. "We made three or four pictures together." Ann found John Wayne to be a charming man and a good father. He used to bring his kids with him on the set. Wayne ate lunch with the grips and the crew and was very loyal to his friends. If John Wayne had a job, his friends had a job. "It didn't surprise me that he became such a big star," Ann continued. "John had an aura about him — a presence. The only other man I knew who had that was Clark Gable."

"She was Gene Autry's first leading lady, too," Al added.

"That's right," Ann said. "He was my very first kiss. And imagine how I felt when I discovered that he was a married man!" Ann paused a beat. "After me, he only kissed his horse."

We all laughed on cue.

Autry was the first singing cowboy. He wrote many songs,

including "Rudolph the Red-Nosed Reindeer" and "Back in the Saddle Again." Ann said that when they made *The Singing Vagabond* together, even after she'd been kidnapped by the bad guys, Gene still had time to sing a song or two. "They tried to make John Wayne a singing cowboy, too," Ann said. "But that didn't work at all." She gave her head two big shakes. "You would not want to hear that."

When Ann and Gene first started making pictures together, Gene knew absolutely nothing about riding a horse. Ann knew more than he did. Gene had never worked in pictures before; the studio pulled him right out of radio. On their first picture together, Gene made a hundred dollars a week, and his sidekick Smiley Burnette was making fifty. Ann earned a hundred and fifty a week because she had an agent, and Gene didn't. "And that's the only time I ever made more money than Gene Autry!" Ann laughed. Ann added that next to Mickey Rooney, Smiley Burnette was the most musically talented man she ever knew. Burnett used to play the accordion that he called his Stomach Steinway.

When Gene was about ninety, Ann sat with him at a big event celebrating Clayton Moore's eightieth birthday. Moore had played the Lone Ranger on television. According to Ann, Gene hated getting old and used to use Grecian Formula in his hair. "It looked pretty bad," she said. During the party, Gene leaned over to Ann and whispered, "I want to talk with you." It sounded important. Ann couldn't imagine what was on his mind. Gene waited till everyone got up to dance, then asked Ann to join him over in the corner of the room. As they stood beside the curtains, Gene looked furtively to both sides, then said, "Annie, dye your hair!"

Ann laughed at her own story. "Here this old guy with hair the color of eggplant was telling me to color *mine*." She thanked him politely, then explained that women of her age do not look good with stove black hair.

"How did *you* end up at Mascot?" I asked.

Ann lowered her chin, pretending to be ashamed. "Well," she said, "I fibbed about that, too."

"You *did?*" I said, surprised.

Then she changed her voice to sound just like an O'Hara. "Oh, yes I did."

The First Picture

My older sister Judith was the beautiful one. She had long auburn hair and the face of an angel. She was a glorious dancer. I was the other child, the pigeon-toed kid. In 1934, my sister was walking down the street in Hollywood when a man stopped her and asked if she'd like to be a WAMPAS Baby Star. It stands for the Western Association of Motion Pictures Advertisers. In the twenties and early thirties, WAMPAS chose about a dozen or so young women a year and gave them big advertising campaigns as the girls closest to stardom. My sister said yes, and they took her to Chicago. Betty Grable was in the same crop of WAMPAS Baby Stars as my sister.

One morning the phone rang at home, and I answered it. The secretary on the other end of the line said that she was calling from MGM Studios. She wanted to speak with Judith Arlen. That was the name my sister had made up for herself. Judith had already done a couple of pictures, including Madam Satan for Cecil B. DeMille and one with Joan Crawford. Well, my sister wasn't home, so I said, "This is she."

The secretary said that the studio was preparing to make a picture called Student Tour. It was about a bunch of young people who were getting their college educations on board ship. They would film in various locations like Catalina. Jimmy Durante would star. Monte Blue and Nelson Eddy were also in it. The woman asked if I'd like to come out to the studio, and I said, "I certainly would!" With that, I changed my dress, brushed my hair, and rode the bus out to MGM. It wasn't far from where we lived. What did I have to lose? Only after I got the job did I tell them that I wasn't Judith. I used the name Joan Arlen. I remember when we took publicity stills for the picture I was one of a bevy of girls surrounding Jimmy Durante. I purposefully positioned myself right beside him and twirled his hair so that he'd look at me — and I would be the focus of the photograph.

When I finished Student Tour, nothing happened. I went back to doing radio. Then one day at the station someone came up to me during intermission and said I had a phone call. I was nervous that something had happened to my mother or my grandmother. When I picked up the phone, the man on the other end of the line introduced himself as John Lancaster. He claimed to be a producer and asked if I wanted to get into pictures. He'd seen a photo of me in the radio section of the paper and thought I looked like Anne Darling. She was a leading lady at Mascot and had recently eloped with an important insurance man who was much older than she and didn't want his new trophy wife to make any more pictures. Mr. Lancaster said that Mascot was looking for a replacement. They were getting ready to shoot a picture called Waterfront Lady and needed the waterfront lady.

Well! I had read enough Kathleen Norris books to know that there were dirty old men out there who asked teenage girls if they wanted to be in the "movies." I knew all about that! I said, "Sir, thank you very much for calling, but I'm not interested." Still he persisted. I didn't want to hang up on him and be rude. My mother had taught me better than that. So I said, "Uh oh. They're waving for me. I have to hang up now, sir. Good-bye." I must have told him three or four times that I had to go. Finally, I politely hung up.

That evening, when I roller skated home from the station, guess who was waiting for me in the living room with my mother. That man!

When he'd read my name in the paper, he thought, I'll bet Rutherford is her real name. No one in her right mind would make up a name like Rutherford. It's too long for a marquee. So he started calling all the Rutherfords in the phone book to see if anyone had a daughter in radio.

I stepped into the living room and took a seat. My mother, who was an excellent judge of character, had already served him some tea. "This is Mr. John Lancaster," she said. "He's a retired producer, but wants to begin working again. And he would like to have you as a client. Tomorrow morning at eight thirty, he will pick us up and take us to Mascot Pictures — it's in the valley — to see a man who's making a picture called Waterfront Lady. *He wants you to meet Mr. Levine, the owner of the studio." My mother explained that they couldn't use minors because that would call for a teacher on the set. If you were younger than eighteen, you could only work four hours a day, and the studio didn't want to limit the number of hours I could work. "So," my mother said, "you'll have to — I'll let you fib this time — you'll have to say you're eighteen." I beamed at her. "Oh, goodie!"*

The next morning, Mr. Lancaster picked us up. I wore a blue summer dress and my sister's heels. My mother let me wear lipstick. When we arrived at Mascot, my mother stayed in the car while Mr. Lancaster and I went upstairs to meet Mr. Levine. He asked how old I was, and I looked him straight in the eye and told him I was eighteen. The men asked me to step outside for a moment while they discussed some things, then pretty soon I returned, and Mr. Levine offered me a job. And since I was now an "adult," I signed my own contract!

When I got back in the car, I bubbled with the details to my mother. She was the most shocked woman in the world. Nothing had ever been planned for me. And here I'm coming home with a movie contract! Suddenly I'm playing with Gene Autry in his first pictures. Then I'm paired with John Wayne. What did I know? I was a kid. I just stuffed a lot of Kleenex in my bra and said, "I'm a leading lady!"

In those days, most pictures were made in eleven days. If it was a big feature, they made it in fourteen. We shot a six-day week. If we were on location, we shot seven. I think the reason they took us on location was so they could work us seven straight days. At that time we didn't have the protection of the Screen Actors Guild. It wasn't until the forties that it became a five-day week.

Those early pictures were made on a dead run. To save money, they cranked them out as fast as they could. There were virtually no rehearsals, except for hurrying through your scenes for the cameraman. If you stumbled on your lines, you didn't get a second chance unless you really flubbed. I remember when we made the serial The Fighting Marines *there was a scene where I was supposed to drive one of those big old-fashioned touring cars. I told the director that I didn't drive. "That's OK," he said. "I'll put a guy on the floor. You steer, and he'll drive." So, this man crouched down on the floor, leaned on the gas, and we took off. Pretty soon, I hit a giant bump, and the guy came flying up. The director left it in the picture! He said it happened so fast that no one would notice. It was on to the next scene.*

Shooting on location was no picnic. They shot in dusty places, and we stayed in rotten little motels. You were always dirty. There was no restaurant. They brought out a chuck wagon and cooked up your meals. I'd have to get up at four in the morning because they started shooting at the crack of dawn. The cry we heard all day was, "Fighting light! Fighting light!" That meant hurry up; the sun's going down. Get the shot in the can. Sometimes the actors would get what we called klieg eyes — sore red eyes from those big klieg lights. So, they'd put thin slices of cold, raw potatoes over the actors' eyes. The prop man carried around potatoes.

Since I didn't drive, every morning a studio car picked me up at home and took me back at midnight. Oftentimes, it was two o'clock in the morning before I left the studio, and I had to be back by six a.m. Once when I had the flu and told the director that I was sick and needed to rest, all he said was, "Sleep fast."

In twelve months, I made more than ten pictures for the studio. Then one day in the summer of 1936, my mother took a good look at me in broad daylight. I had huge circles under my eyes. Actually, I had circles under my circles. "That's enough!" she cried. And she marched me downtown to the Los Angeles courthouse, said I'd lied about my age, and had my contract dissolved. At first, they weren't quite sure what to do with me. It was quite contrary to court customs. Every year, hundreds of girls under the age of twenty-one would appear in court for approval of their screen contracts. They'd met very few who asked to get out of one.

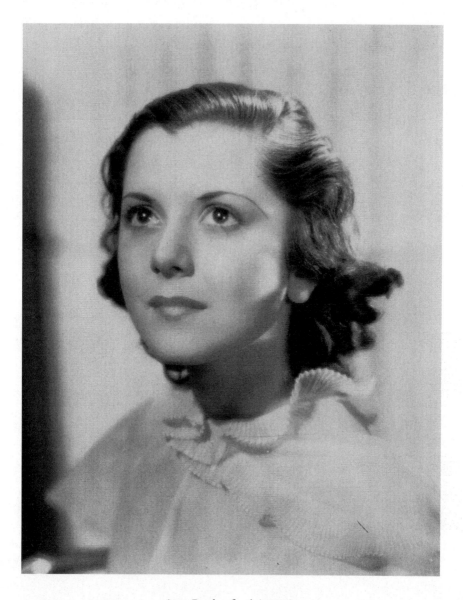

Ann Rutherford (1935)
— photo courtesy of the James Bawden Collection

Ann in *Waterfront Lady* (1935)
— photo courtesy of the James Bawden Collection

Ann in *Public Cowboy No. 1* (1937)
— photo courtesy of the James Bawden Collection

Ann Rutherford (1935)
— photo courtesy of the James Bawden Collection

Ann Rutherford with costar Russell Hardie in *Down to the Sea* (1936)
for Republic Pictures
— photo courtesy of the James Bawden Collection

Ann Rutherford at the Los Angeles Courthouse to terminate her contract
with Republic Pictures (1936)
— photo courtesy of the James Bawden Collection

The Letters

Be smart, but never show it.
— *Louis B. Mayer*

"I followed my sister's advice," Ann said, as Heidi, Al, and I listened on backstage. "Never say no. No matter what the studio asks you to do, say you can do it. And that's what I did. Meanwhile, I'd be out taking lessons in whatever it was I said I could do. My motto was: Fake it till you make it. I figured if I could just get one day's work on the picture, it would cost them too much to replace me."

When asked if she could ride, Ann said, "I've ridden for years." She didn't know how. While working on *Murder in the Music Hall*, they asked if she could ice skate, and Ann said, "Of course I can ice skate." She never had. On the same picture, they asked if she knew how to fence. "Absolutely," Ann replied. She'd never fenced either. So, she found a fencing instructor on Highland Avenue and took a two-hour lesson. When Ann got around to reading the script, she discovered, to her great surprise, that she was supposed to ice skate and fence at the same time! "That," Ann said, "wasn't easy." Ann grinned at me and shrugged. "They weren't harmful fibs. And everything worked out just fine."

"Tell him who taught you how to swim," Al interjected.

"Oh, yes. After *Waterfront Lady*, I made ..." Ann paused to remember the title.

"*Down to the Sea*," Al helped out.

"Yes, in *Down to the Sea* I played a Greek fisherman's daughter. They asked if I could swim underwater, and I said of course. But the truth was I didn't have a clue. I could barely wade. After I looked at the script, I went into absolute shock. There was a scene where my part dives off the boat, and a young man dives off his, then we chase each other underwater. Well, I thought, I'll never be able to pull *this* off. The next day, I grabbed my bathing suit and script, stuffed them into a bag, and walked toward Sunset Boulevard. I remembered seeing an athletic club in the area. Surely they'd have a pool. Eventually I found the club, walked inside to the front desk, and asked to see the swimming instructor. They said that the club was for men only. Disappointed, I started out of the building when suddenly this blonde angel appeared in the doorway. I'd seen him before. A few years earlier, my girlfriends and I had gone to the '32 Olympics and watched him swim. I walked right up to him and said, 'I know *you*. You're Buster Crabbe.' "

My eyes bulged. "*Tarzan?*"

"Yes! He was just so cute, just darling. I thought — *he'll* be able to teach me how to swim. I hurled myself at this poor unfortunate soul, told him that I'd lied my way into a picture, and asked him if he'd be willing to teach me." Ann shook her head at herself. "I had the nerve of a burglar. Then I pulled out my dog-eared script and showed him where it said I needed to swim underwater. He walked me over to a bench and said, 'Sit down here. I'll be right back.' And then he left. About ten minutes later, he returned and said, 'OK, kid, I can teach you.' When I asked him how he managed it, he said he'd cleared out the whole pool." Ann beamed. "So, Buster Crabbe taught me how to swim. After three days, I could swim backwards and forwards and sideways and upside-down. You would have thought I was Esther Williams!"

The studio waited to film Ann's underwater swimming scene till the last day. Mascot didn't have a pool, so they drove Ann to Universal Studios. When they stopped the car, Ann got out, but didn't see any pool, only a giant wooden water tower. Up on the platforms that circled the tank, cameras were already positioned in front of the portholes. Horrified, Ann cried, "You expect me to swim in *that?*" No one had told her. "Before I agree to do this," Ann said, "I want to see what it's going to be like. And if I'm going to climb up there, I want a big guy in front of me and another behind." So they sandwiched her between two big men, and the three of them climbed up the long ladder. When Ann looked inside the tank, she saw that they'd fixed it up with phony seaweed and coral, but there was no spit rail. "I'm an excellent underwater swimmer," Ann said, "but when I come up, I need something to hold onto." She suggested that they hang phony seaweed every six inches so she'd have something to grab when she emerged. It took some time, but she shot the scene.

After leaving Republic, Ann's agent started making the rounds at other studios with canisters of Ann's pictures under his arms. Ann made *The Devil is Driving* with Richard Dix at Columbia and two shorts (*Annie Laurie* and *Carnival in Paris*) at MGM. Metro liked what they saw and in 1937 signed Ann to a seven-year contract at $300 a week. (The studio loaned her right back to Republic for *Public Enemy No. 1.*) At that time, most young contract players were signed at $50 to $75 a week. "I wasn't only rich," Ann said brightly. "I was well to do! But the studio could drop me after any six-month period, so I had to make good."

Ann was thrilled to be at MGM. At that time, Metro was known as the Tiffany of the studios. "It ruled the roost," Ann said. "And to be there was a deep compliment." There were other studios — 20th Century-Fox, RKO Radio, Columbia, Warner Brothers, Universal, and Paramount — and all had stars, but none as many as MGM. When Ann signed her contract, MGM's star roster included Greta Garbo, Lionel Barrymore, Clark Gable, Norma Shearer, William Powell, Myrna Loy, Robert Taylor, Jean Harlow, Robert Montgomery, James Stewart, Mickey Rooney, and Jackie Cooper. And the list kept growing. "Warners had its stock company," Ann said, "but who'd want to rub elbows with the likes of Guy Kibbee and Hugh Herbert, bless their hearts?"

When Ann joined MGM's ranks, the studio was enjoying a banner year. Four of its stars (Clark Gable, Robert Taylor, William Powell, and Myrna Loy) hit the top-ten list, more than any other studio. Of the sixteen top grossing films of 1937, most were made at MGM, including *Personal Property* with Jean Harlow and Robert Taylor, *Saratoga* with Gable and Harlow (she died during filming), and *The Good Earth* with Paul Muni and Luise Rainer. At the Academy Awards, MGM nabbed both the Best Actor and Best Actress awards with Rainer's performance in *The Good Earth* and Spencer Tracy's in *Captains Courageous*. The year also marked the screen debut of new find Lana Turner.

Metro-Goldwyn-Mayer got right to work on its new starlet. The hair and makeup departments restyled Ann's hair and reshaped her eyebrows. She had nice teeth, so they didn't need to be capped or whitened. The studio created a fake biography for her in which they said she'd started acting at the age of four in San Francisco. They shaved three years off of her age. From then on, Ann said she was born in 1920, though she was actually born in 1917. Metro didn't change her name as they did with so many of their contract players.

Ann's first name sounded sweet, and her last name had class. The combination of the two flowed well together. Soon, the publicity department began to supply stories, fashion spreads, and cheesecake photos of their new acquisition to the fan magazines. Though Ann was beautiful and shapely, she would not be presented as a young siren, but as the girl next door — the All-American Sweetheart.

For Ann, MGM was like a finishing school. The studio taught their newcomers how to work with hair and makeup, dress, pose, sit, and walk: Suck in your stomach and square your shoulders. They gave their contractees voice, dance, diction, fencing, and riding lessons and coached them in how to conduct an interview — be careful what you say and always promote your newest picture. "They constantly worked with you," Ann said. "It was like being in a nursery where they weeded, hoed, and watered every day. If you had two left feet, they gave you dance lessons. If you walked peculiarly, they put books on your head. If your eyes squinted, they even had someone to help you fix that." And the studio looked after their talent. Through its special services department, each contract player was assigned an aide who arranged publicity appointments, booked their travel, and took care of errands. If you needed to renew your driver's license or register to vote, they handled that, too.

One of Ann's first assignments at Metro was a Joan Crawford picture titled *The Bride Wore Red*. The production values at MGM were hugely different from what Ann had been used to. "Mascot was considered Poverty Row," Ann said. "They didn't even give you a still of the picture you just finished." Ann recalled freezing her tail off when she shot *The Bride Wore Red*. Crawford demanded that the soundstage be air cooled because she tended to perspire a lot. In the summer, they put ice on the top of her soundstages to keep them cool for her.

As the four of us chatted in the hallway, I noticed that the crowd had started to dwindle. Heidi and I decided it was time to get going. Hugs and handshakes went around. I thanked Ann one last time and told her that I could have listened to her all night long. She squeezed my hand and said, "Thank you, Phil. It's nice to be remembered."

When I got back to the Bay Area, one of the first things I did was research Ann online. Ann was born Mary Cecilia Ramone Theresa Ann Rutherford on November 2. I smiled when I saw that we almost shared the same birthday. In one interview, when asked her age, Ann said, "I celebrate, but don't count." In another, she advised, "Women no longer sit and rock, so get up, clamp yourself together, and get cracking. Don't think of the number of years in your life. Think of the life in your years." I could hear her saying that.

Three weeks after Ann's birth, her family moved from Canada to the United States. Her mother, Lucille Mansfield, had been a coloratura soprano and won the title of Miss Arizona before it became a state. Ann's father, John Rutherford, was a tenor with the Metropolitan Opera, who sang under the name of John Guilberty. He was fourteen years his wife's senior. The two met on tour and eloped. When Ann was five, her parents separated. A few years later, Lucille took the girls to San Francisco, where they lived for a couple of years before moving to Los Angeles. Ann's grandmother also came to live with them. One of their first homes in Southern California was a small apartment in Hollywood. Ann attended Virgil Junior High, then Los Angeles and Fairfax High Schools.

I discovered varying reports on Ann's birthplace. Ann revealed the reason for this discrepancy in an interview she gave later in life, when she decided to "come clean." Early in her career, a reporter had asked her where she was born. Ann had never really liked the sound of

Vancouver, her true birthplace. "It was the *ouver* in Vancouver that didn't appeal to me," Ann explained. But she loved the name of the city where her father was born: Toronto. So she said she was born there. Many years later when she visited Toronto, she saw a wall listing local celebrities. On it hung Ann's picture right beside Mary Pickford's. Above their names were with the words, "Local Girls Make Good." Ann felt so ashamed.

Back home, I wrote Ann a letter telling her how wonderful it had been to meet her. I'd found her Beverly Hills address online. Along with the letter, I sent an inscribed copy of my new book and a stamped envelope in case she wanted to reply. Weeks and then months went by, but I never heard from her. A couple of times, I contacted people who ran her fan sites, but I never got a response. I hoped Ann was OK.

A few years later, I accepted a teaching position at the American International School in Budapest. I had taught overseas before. The first time I went abroad, I joked that I got my sign to move from a spider. I'd been teaching for fifteen years in California public schools. Every year, I read *Charlotte's Web* to my grade-schoolers, and each time I'd get choked up when Charlotte the spider died. Well, one year I finished reading the book and didn't shed a tear, not even a sniffle. I knew then that it was time for a change.

As I was packing to leave for Budapest, I came across the cocktail napkin that Ann had signed for me at the Roosevelt Hotel and slid it in a folder of important papers. When I got to Hungary, I framed it along with her picture.

At the end of each school year, I'd fly back to California to see family and friends and also check on my house, which I was renting out. In the summer of 2010, my tenants handed me a brown grocery bag full of mail. Figuring it was mostly junk, I threw it in the trunk of my car to look at later. On my last day before flying back to Hungary, I started opening the mail. Halfway through the bag, I pulled out a pink envelope. It was handwritten to me. The penmanship was elegant. *What's this?* When I read the return address, my heart flipped. It was from Beverly Hills! From Ann Rutherford! Immediately I tore open the envelope and started reading.

Dear Phillip,

I can't believe that it has taken me so very long to acknowledge your wonderful book and congratulate you on what you have done. I have since bought ten copies and given them to special friends. I have just ordered ten more.

Now for the reason it took me so long to get back to you … I had been traveling around the globe for Gone With the Wind. *When I returned from each trip, I'd pay the bills, change my clothes, and take off again. Meanwhile, the pile of manila envelopes grew taller, but I just didn't have time to "do fan mail." That is where your envelope ended up.*

One day a stack fell over, and as I picked everything up, I noticed that one of the envelopes was fatter than the others. It held a book. Then when I saw the date and realized that you had sent it to me long ago, I nearly had a fit. I recalled our encounter clearly and remembered our visit.

Had I been home when your letter arrived, I would have responded right away. But the person who sorted the mail simply put it on the wrong pile. Actually, it's sort of spooky the way it made itself known to me.

Anyway, I am pleased and proud that I know you and hope you are doing book signings and having fun with "your" fans. Oh, I have tried to phone you (I called information), but the nice lady who answers says it's her number, not yours.

> *With Admiration and Love,*
> *Ann*

My hands were shaking. Below her signature Ann included her phone number. *Does she want me to call her?* Quickly I checked the date. Ann had mailed the letter twelve months before. It had been sitting in the bag for over a year!

After reading the letter two more times, I began going through the rest of the mail. At the bottom of the bag I discovered a *second* pink envelope! *Another one?* I checked the return address. Ann sent it a month after the first.

Dear Phil,

First of all, go straight to the head of the class! Then, please send me your phone number! Information gave me a number that no longer works. I have just ordered ten more copies of your book for people who love kids and don't mind laughing out loud. Call me!

> *Love and Hugs,*
> *Ann*

With the letters in my lap, I drove to my mom's home where I was staying, and ran into the house, hollering. My mother came rushing down the stairs, and I told her what had happened and read the letters aloud. My mom was as surprised as I was. She remembered Ann from *Gone With the Wind*, of course, and the Andy Hardy pictures.

"Why do you think she wants me to call her?" I asked, flabbergasted.

To my mother, the answer was clear. "Phil, you've connected with your hearts," she said. "You opened yours when writing the book, and she opened hers making all those movies. Now that she's read your writing, she feels that she knows you."

I thought about it for a second. Then I picked up the phone and put it against my chest. "What in the world do I say to a movie star?"

"Just be yourself," my mom said. "And for God's sake, breathe!"

I took a deep Lamaze breath, dialed Ann's number, and anxiously counted the rings. After the tenth one, someone picked up.

"Hello?" a woman's voice answered.

"Hello." I cleared my throat. "I'm ... I'm calling for Ann Rutherford, please."

"May I tell her who's calling?" She sounded skeptical.

"Yes. My name is Phillip Done. I'm a teacher and a writer. Miss Rutherford wrote to me some time ago asking me to call her and ..."

"... Well, it's about time!" the voice cried. It was Ann. "I thought you were mad at me!"

"*Mad?* Good heavens, *no!*"

After I explained what had happened and Ann explained why it had taken her so long to get back to me, we started chatting like old friends. My mom was right. Hearts connected.

"I could have kicked myself for opening my mail so late," I said. "If I'd read your letter earlier, I would have driven down to see you."

"I might not have been in town," Ann replied.

Ann had just returned from speaking at Kent State University to raise money for its Katharine Hepburn costume collection. Unbeknownst to anyone, Katharine had saved many of her performance clothes. When she passed away, they were discovered in an upstairs closet. Her executors gave them to the university. After receiving the costumes, the school needed to raise money to care for them, so they decided to host some fundraisers. They wanted to bring in a celebrity who could pull in an audience, and one of the committee members suggested Ann Rutherford. They were friends. "But I'll warn you," he said, "she's the type of person who if you ask what time it is, will tell you how to make a clock."

"The first time I went out to Kent State," Ann said, "I stood on the stage, and the host asked his first question. I turned to the audience and started talking. An hour later, I was *still* answering." Ann spoke over my snickers. "I realized I talked a lot, but I didn't know I talk *that* much." *

"Do a lot of places invite you to speak?" I asked.

"Oh, yes. I can't go to all the places that ask me. There are just too many. Last year alone, I must have spoken at seven or eight different festivals. They roll me out and prop me up on stage. I've been disinterred." Ann continued as I chuckled. "You know something. Some people's pasts rise up to haunt them. Mine has risen up to bless me."

What a lovely thought

"What kinds of things do people ask you about?" I asked.

"Oh, they ask if I enjoyed working in pictures. And everyone wants to hear about *The Wind*."

I smiled. I'd never heard it referred to as *The Wind* before.

"Of course, they all want to know what it was like to work with Clark Gable and Vivien Leigh and David Selznick. You know, there aren't many of us left from the cast anymore. The woman who played Maybelle Merriwether is still alive. Mary Anderson is her name. She lives here in California. You can't get her to attend anything. She won't budge. She's a card-carrying idiot. I've done

---

* In a 1941 interview with Ann conducted at the MGM commissary, a reporter wrote, "Ann speaks at a rate of 400 words per minute." At the end of the interview, Ann said, "Please don't call me a chatterbox! I know I am, but I can't help it."

everything but insult her to get her to come and speak about the picture. One year, a festival for *The Wind* was coming up, and I heard that she wasn't coming. So I called her and said, 'Mary, can you stand up?' She said yes. I said, 'Can you put one foot in front of the other?' Again she said yes. 'Then you can go!' I said. That same year, Scarlett on the Square — it's a museum in Marietta, Georgia — sent her a stack of programs to sign for one of their events, thinking that if she wouldn't come, maybe she'd give her autograph. Well, I thought I'd have to send the law out to get them back. Mary never signed them." Ann gave a sigh. "I'll never understand people like that. She doesn't know the warmth you get from having been part of *The Wind*. I believe there comes a point in life when you get as far as you possibly can with all the steam you have left in your system. When you get that far, it falls upon you to just live graciously."

Ann couldn't see the big smile on my face.

"And, of course, Aunt Olivia's still with us," Ann continued.

"*Aunt* Olivia?" I said, confused.

"Yes. Olivia de Havilland."

"Why do you call her *Aunt* Olivia?"

"Because she's in the family. My second husband, Bill Dozier, was first married to Joan Fontaine, Olivia's sister. They had a child named Deborah, who is my stepdaughter. Her aunt is Olivia."

"So, let me get this straight," I said. "In *Gone With the Wind*, you and Olivia are related by marriage. So, that means you're family on *and* off the screen."

"Yes."

"Does Olivia go to the *Gone With the Wind* events, too?"

"No. She lives in Paris. That's a long trip. Besides, Livvie spends all of her time working on her autobiography. She's doing all the research, writing every word herself. She has volumes of scrapbooks and papers all over her house. She's been working on that damn book for thirty years. Frankly, I don't think she'll ever finish."

"Have you ever thought of writing a book?"

"I've been approached several times, but I just don't have the time. I'm too busy living my life. Besides, you know how those celebrity biographies are. So often they end up saying bad things about people. I wouldn't want to say anything bad."

Darling, I thought.

"If I ever do decide to write a book," Ann said, "I know what I'd call it — *Riding the Wind.*"

"Great title."

"It sums up my life."

"When making *Gone* ... I mean *The Wind* ... did you know it was going to be classic?"

"We had no *clue.* Actually, I take that back. Rand Brooks knew. He played Scarlett's first husband, Charles Hamilton. He knew it would be for the ages. He sensed it. The rest of us had no idea. You see, at that time everyone in town said the picture was going right down the drain. Selznick's folly, they called it. We had no idea it would be such a sensation. In those days, a movie ran a year. Maybe two, tops. Then they made guitar picks out of it. I never dreamed it would endure like it has. It's become like a person, an entity. In my lifetime, there has never been a film that has captured the imagination like *Gone With the Wind.* If you had told me in 1939 that almost seventy-five years later, I'd be attending events for *The Wind,* I would have thought you were off your rocker.

"For me," Ann continued, "the special part in all this is that with each generation a whole new group of young people is touched by the picture. It's like Mickey Mouse. As long as there are little children, there will always be Mickey Mouse. On an adult level, *Gone*

With the Wind does that. When my great-niece was thirteen, she swapped me her *Harry Potter* book for *Gone With the Wind*. She read it just like I had. She cried and cried and couldn't put it down. I never got it back."

Chuckling, I asked, "So how did you come to be cast as Scarlett's youngest sister?"

"Honey, I haven't told you *that*?"

"No."

"I didn't even test for it." Ann's laugh sparkled through the receiver. "Well, you've heard of some people getting a job by the skin of their teeth. I got that part by a *hair* — a hair on my eyebrows."

The Eyebrows

*M*y *mother and I were on the 20th Century Limited traveling from New York to Los Angeles. We were just leaving the dining car after lunch. As we walked down the corridor through the aperture, that little section where the two cars hook up, I spotted David Selznick coming toward me. He was a tall, broad-shouldered man. David and I didn't know each other well, but he certainly knew who I was.*

I said to my mother, "You go on ahead. I'll be with you in a minute." And I waited there like a spider. At that time, everyone in Hollywood — in the country — knew that David was casting Gone With the Wind. *I had already read the book twice and was crazy about it. We all were. As soon as I finished reading it, I went back to the first page and started over. I had read that David paid $50,000 for the film rights. Well, I had some advice to give to Mr. Selznick.*

When David cleared the door and saw me, his eyes rolled heavenward, then he looked longingly toward the dining car. I'm sure he thought I was going to ask to audition for the picture, but I wasn't even thinking about that. It never even occurred to me.

"Hello, Miss Rutherford," he said, touching the brim of his hat.

"Hello, Mr. Selznick." Then, without any warning, I clutched this poor guy by both arms and said, "Look at my eyebrows! Look at them!" He looked down obediently. "In Gone With the Wind," *I said, "Scarlett*

is described as having eyebrows like bird's wings. No woman had tweezers back then. Only doctors had tweezers."

David listened as I carried on. By then I think I had let go of his arms.

"Mr. Selznick," I went on, "I've been in New York for the past three weeks, and my eyebrows have almost grown back. But as soon as I get back to Metro, Jack Dawn (the head of the makeup department) is going to reach into his vest pocket, pull out his tweezers, and start plucking them out. Mr. Dawn is a maniac about it. And each time he plucks them, they grow back with less enthusiasm. They get very discouraged. Pretty soon I'm going to have to draw those silly little lines on my forehead like Marlene Dietrich!"

Then I pointed right at him. "I want you to tell your makeup men to throw their tweezers away and stop picking ladies' eyebrows out. In the 1860s, women had to bite their lips and pinch their cheeks to make them blush. They did not pluck their eyebrows. And besides, actors need their eyebrows. I can't show that I'm angry or upset or sad unless I can frown or pull my brows together." Then I scrunched them really hard to make my point. "See!"

David nodded seriously and thanked me. Then he reached into his pocket, took out a pen and a card, and scribbled something on it. "Ann," he said, "I am very grateful to you. I had not thought of that." As he pushed the door to go into the dining car, David turned around and quite floridly thanked me a second time. Looking back on that day, I can't believe I spoke to him like that. I didn't know any better. Nobody had ever taught me how to act with a producer.

Years later, when David was at my house for a party, I asked whatever possessed him to give me the part of Carreen. "Well," he said, "I had just signed Barbara O'Neil to play Ellen O'Hara. When you accosted me on the train ..." We both laughed when he mentioned that. "... all I could see was your nose. It was straight like Barbara O'Neil's. I *hadn't cast any of the O'Hara daughters yet. I thought — if I can't get Shirley Temple and I can't get Judy Garland because she'll be making that damn Oz picture forever, I'll bet I can get Ann Rutherford to play Scarlett's youngest sister. Yes — she can do it." **

---

* On February 15, 1939, after seeing her first photos of Barbara O'Neil and Ann Rutherford, Margaret Mitchell wrote a letter to Marcella Rabwin at Selznick International Pictures expressing how pleased she was that Carreen looked so much like Mrs. O'Hara. Miss Mitchell found the similarities "beautifully subtle."

The Call

Forget it, Louis! No Civil War picture ever made a nickel!

— *Irving Thalberg*

With Ann's two letters safely in my carry-on, the next morning I flew to Europe. When I got back to Budapest, I pulled out my movie books and read up on *Gone With the Wind*. Released in 1939, this star-studded epic is undoubtedly one of the most popular films of all time. It is also one of the first feature films to be shot in color, and with a running time of three hours and forty-two minutes, is one of the longest films to date. The picture received ten Academy Awards and is ranked fourth on the American Film Institute's list of Top 100 Best American Films of All Time. Since its release, the picture has made $400 million in theater receipts, approximately $3.3 billion in current ticket prices. Some estimates claim that one out of every three people in the United States has seen it, and that more people have watched *Gone With the Wind* than any other picture.

Soon after I returned to Hungary, I gave Ann a call. She had told me that she didn't do e-mail. "I don't compute," she once said. When I asked her what the best way to keep in touch was, she cried, "Just pick up the phone!"

Ann was out when I called, so I left a voice message with my

Hungarian number. The next evening, the phone rang.

"Hello," I said, picking up.

"Hello. This is the operator. I have Ann Rutherford on the line. Will you accept the call?"

An operator-assisted call? To *Europe?* I'd only seen those in the movies and didn't know they even did that anymore. "Yes. Yes," I said. "I'll take the call."

"Phil," Ann's voice came on the line, "is that *you?*"

"Yes. Why did you make an operator-assisted call?"

"Your number was so *long!*"

I laughed out loud.

"I'm thinking of getting one of those iPhones," Ann said. "You can put everyone's number in it, and when you want to make a call, all you have to do is press a button."

Ann asked about my new crop of third-graders, where they were from and what they were learning. She was genuinely interested, which tickled me. I told her they were studying the continents and where Hungary was located.

I asked Ann if she'd been to Budapest, and she said she hadn't. The closest she'd been was Vienna. One evening while she was there, Ann stood on a street corner waiting for a taxi when a woman started yelling at her and shooing Ann away. It wasn't till Ann was in the cab that she realized why. The woman thought Ann was invading her "territory."

"How's your writing coming along?" Ann asked.

"Don't ask," I said with a groan. "Since my last book, I've written two manuscripts, but my agent has had trouble selling them. Publishing has changed so much in the last few years. It's not enough to write a good book anymore. Apparently, now you have to have this enormous platform — a TV show, a radio program, or a regular column. Bottom line — I'm just not famous enough." I let out a long breath. "I'm afraid I might be done as a writer."

"Dear," Ann said, "you mustn't give up. I love your writing. You don't embellish. You don't use too many adjectives."

"Thanks," I half-laughed.

Then Ann told me about her friend A. C. Lyles. He had always wanted to work in the movie business. As a teenager, Lyles started selling handbills at a Paramount theater in Indiana. One day, Adolph Zukor — he owned Paramount — went out to visit the theater, and there he met Lyles. "I'm going to grow up and be a producer at your studio," Lyles told him. After Zukor's visit, Lyles wrote a letter to Mr. Zukor every week. When Lyles turned eighteen, he took all of his money and bought a one-way ticket to Los Angeles. As soon as he arrived, he headed straight to Paramount and said to the guard, "Call Mr. Zukor's office and tell him that A. C. Lyles is here." When the secretaries heard that Lyles was at the gate, they squealed. They'd been reading his letters for months. They dragged Lyles up to see Zukor and begged him to give Lyles a job. Zukor hired him as a messenger boy. Lyles worked his way up the lot, and today there's a building at Paramount named after him. "He's been at Paramount for eighty years," Ann said. "And why? Because he never gave up."

I pushed a smile. It was sweet of her to encourage me like this.

"Honey, when is your next time off?" Ann asked.

"Mmm ... the last week in October. It's fall break. Why?"

"Come see me."

"*Really?*" I said, perking up.

"Yes. You come out here, and I'll take you to the Polo Lounge. I have a favorite table outside. We can sit and gossip. Then we'll go dancing in the streets."

Adorable.

"I'd love that," I said.

"And when you come out to California, I'll give you the egg cartons."

"*Egg* cartons?"

"For your students. Don't you need egg cartons for crafts and things?"

"Yes," I chuckled. "But ..."

"Well, I've already started collecting them for you. I go through a lot of eggs. I'm very fond of loose scrambled eggs. I make them myself. I have a few cottage cheese containers for you, too, and have threatened everybody if they dare throw them out. Oh, and do you have any copies of your book you can spare? I've been handing them out to all my friends. Everyone just loves it. Your mother must be bursting with pride."

I laughed. "Sure, I'll bring you some copies."

Ann grabbed her engagement book, and we planned my trip. I'd stay with my friend Paul in Santa Monica and visit Ann a couple of times during the week. Beverly Hills wasn't far. When we finished discussing the details, I told Ann that I had been reading up on *Gone With the Wind* and asked how old she was when she made the picture.

"Eighteen," she answered. "But I could play thirteen. Carreen's first line in the picture is, 'Can't I stay up for the barbecue? I'm thirteen now.' Back then, when actors signed with the studio, we were taught that if people inquired about our age to just say, 'How old do you *want* me to be?' " Ann paused for a giggle. "It's funny. When you start out in life, you lie *up* to get the job, and later in life, you lie *down*, so to speak." *

That made me laugh.

"Actually," Ann said, "I'm glad that I got the part of Carreen and not Suellen. When Scarlett smacked her across the face, that must have really hurt."

I laughed again.

"When it was announced that Selznick bought the movie rights," Ann went on, "everyone was casting the picture. It became a nation-wide topic of conversation — a dinner sport on par with Roosevelt's election. We were all talking about it. Who would play Rhett? Who would be Scarlett?"

"So, after you spoke with Selznick on the train, did he just call Metro and ask for you?"

"Yes," Ann replied. "But Mr. Mayer was absolutely against it."

---

* Ann was in fact twenty-one when she filmed *Gone With the Wind*. After changing the year of her birth on her studio bio, she always claimed she was eighteen when making the picture.

Miss O'Hara

I was in my dressing room at the studio when I received a phone call from Ida Koverman, Louis B. Mayer's assistant, to go see Mr. Mayer. *Why does he want to see me?* I thought. *Am I in trouble?* It was rare that one got a call from Mr. Mayer's office. If you did, it was usually because you had done something awful the night before at Ciro's! Nervous, I walked to the Thalberg Building and up to Mayer's office, where I waited outside by Mrs. Koverman's desk. Koverman was tall and gray-haired; she wore a pince-nez. She was definitely not the grandmother type. Her nickname on the lot was Mt. Ida. Finally, she said Mr. Mayer would see me. I stood up, adjusted my skirt, and stepped through the giant walnut doors into Mr. Mayer's office.

The room smelled of cigars. Mr. Mayer sat behind a large wraparound desk, his hands clasped over his suit jacket. He was always well dressed. Everything in the room was white — the desk, carpet, chairs, sofas, leather walls, even the grand piano in the corner. His desk, all shiny and polished with silver accent pieces, was elevated on a platform to make him look taller. He was a short man. I was taller than he was.

I walked the long stretch to his desk — it was known as the quarter-mile walk — and Mr. Mayer motioned for me to have a seat.

"Ann," he said, leaning back in his chair, "I wanted to be the first one to tell you. My son-in-law has been trying to borrow you."

"He has?" I said, sitting up. "Who? Which son-in-law?"

Mr. Mayer took off his shell-rimmed glasses and started wiping them with a handkerchief. "David Selznick. He wants to borrow you for his new picture."

I leaned toward him. "What's the name of this picture?" I asked slowly.

"Oh, I don't know," he said, twisting his face. "It has to do with slaves and the Civil War and …"

I sprang out of my chair. "It must be the book! The wonderful book, Gone With the Wind!" I put my hands on his desk. "May I do it?"

"My readers tell me it's a nothing part."

"That doesn't matter. I'll do anything! I'll carry a tray. I'll open a door. I'll hold the horses!"

"Ann, we can't put your name above the title in one of our pictures then lend you out to play a nothing part."

"Oh, please let me do it," I pleaded. "Please!"

Mr. Mayer just shook his head.

Well, I just had to be in that picture. I had to. I'd already begged, and Mr. Mayer wasn't budging. So, I pulled his trick: I burst out crying. Mr. Mayer was a very sentimental man. He was known to get misty-eyed if you asked him what time it was.

As I blubbered away, wiping away the tears with my handkerchief, he finally said, "Oh, for goodness' sakes, Ann, stop your crying. I'll talk to David and see if he can do something better with the part. Now get into your car and drive over to see him."

"Oh, thank you!" I cried.

I ran around Mr. Mayer's desk and threw my arms around him. Then I hurried down the quarter-mile stretch, burst out of the office, and beamed at a very confused Mt. Ida. Little did I know that this tiny role would turn out to be the greatest nothing part I ever had.

Beverly Hills

Don't settle for the little dream; go on to the big one.
— Norman Maine, *A Star Is Born*

October break finally arrived. For weeks, I'd been putting *X*s through the squares on my calendar like kids count the days until Christmas. I flew the fourteen hours from Budapest to Los Angeles, rented a car, and drove to my friend Paul's house in Santa Monica. Beverly Hills was only twenty minutes down the road. The morning I was to meet Ann, I ironed my best shirt, polished my shoes, and tried on three different ties. At the florist, I drove the poor shop owner crazy trying to choose what flowers to buy for a movie star. After about twenty minutes of back and forth, he finally said, "Listen, why don't you just go inside the refrigerator, grab what you want, and make the arrangement yourself." So, I did.

With my bouquet resting on the backseat and Ann's address in my hand, I drove down Wilshire Boulevard to her home. When I passed the brown sign saying *Welcome to Beverly Hills*, goose bumps popped up on my arms.

It's always satisfying when a new place looks like the picture you have in your head. I'd been to Southern California several times, but surprisingly never to Beverly Hills. The city was exactly like I'd pictured: giant lots, tall palm trees, perfectly manicured yards, and enormous iron gates for peeking through. When I found Ann's street, Greenway Drive, I drove slowly along the road looking for her address. Gardeners were out mowing lawns. My face lit up when I spotted Ann's house. It was just as she had described it: a sprawling, white two-story English Georgian with a semicircular driveway leading up to the front door. The golf course for the Beverly Hills Country Club was directly across the street. "You can't miss it," she'd said. "The door is handicap blue."

After I parked and turned off the ignition, I sat in the car for a few minutes before opening the door. I was nervous. Finally, I stepped out and put on my sport coat. The air was warm; it felt good to be back in the California sun. Looking up at the house, I sensed there was something vaguely familiar about it. After thinking about it a second, it occurred to me why. Ann's home looked just like Polly Benedict's white colonial house in the Hardy pictures.

I walked up the driveway to the front steps where a sign above the bell read, "Please wait. It takes me a while to get to the door. But I'm a comin'!" I smiled as I read it. It reminded me of when Dorothy and her gang read, "Bell out of order. Please knock." at the entrance to the Emerald City.

After practicing how I would present the flowers, I knocked on the door. No answer. I knocked a second time. No one came. I sat down on the brick steps beside a potted lemon tree, thinking of what to do next. Soon, a man wearing a tool belt stepped from around the corner. Standing up, I told him that I was waiting for Miss Rutherford. He offered to call her on his cell. When he got her on the phone, he handed it to me.

"Hi, Ann. It's Phil. I'm here at your house."

"I'm on my way, honey. I'm just running some errands." Then Ann started scolding her driver. "I don't know what the address is!

Just follow the steering wheel." Ann got back on the phone. "Honey, I'll be there in a jiffy. Don't go anywhere!"

About fifteen minutes later, a 1962 black Cadillac Coupe de Ville with Batmobile-like back fins pulled slowly into the driveway and up to the front door. Ann was sitting in the passenger seat. I hurried down the steps as Ann's driver got out and opened her door.

"Oh, it's so wonderful to see you!" I said, excited.

"You too, honey." It had been six years since I'd seen her.

I reached out with the bouquet. "These are for you."

"Why, thank you. They're lovely."

I held on to the flowers as I helped Ann out of the car. She wore a red, ruffled blouse. Her hair was pulled back with a scarf that matched. Her red eyeglass frames were covered with rhinestones.

Slowly, we walked arm in arm up the steps. Ann was frailer than the last time I had seen her. She used a cane now. At the front door, she opened her handbag, pulled out her house key, and spoke right to it. "There you are!" Ann turned to me. "I hope you don't mind me talking to myself." Ann gave me a grin. "Sometimes I listen." Then, with a shaky hand, she inserted the key into the lock and pushed open the door.

There are certain moments in a life that become indelibly imprinted on one's mind. This moment, I sensed, was one of them. As Ann and I stepped across the threshold into the large entry with rounded walls, my eyes swept the interior like a follow spot. A white staircase similar to the one where Rhett Butler first eyes Scarlett at Twelve Oaks scrolled up to the second floor. Beyond the entryway, a large sunroom with wall-to-wall sliding glass doors looked out to a massive yard. In the distance, a pool and a pool house. As I took it all in, I felt like William Holden as he first steps into Norma Desmond's mansion on Sunset Boulevard.

"How long have you lived here?" I asked.

"Since 1943."

I quickly did the math. "That's almost seventy years."

"Y-*ep*," she said. "I know the sound of every door and the squeak of every inch of the hardwood floor. It has good bones, this house."

Arms still linked, we stepped under an enormous chandelier dripping with large, cut crystals.

"That's beautiful," I said, looking up.

She pointed at it with her cane. "It's a big pain to dust."

Together, we padded through the entry and into the sunroom where light streamed through the windows onto the tiled floor, glass-topped tables, and retro pink vinyl chairs. Stacks of mail sat on the tables. As we walked through the room, I glanced at some of the return addresses: *Chicago, Honolulu, London, Mumbai, Beijing.*

Ann said it was all fan mail. Every day the Rubbermaid tub under the mail slot was full. Some days she received as many as fifty fan letters. "I'm drowning in them," she said. "Everyone wants a photo or an autograph." Ann didn't have a secretary anymore. It was difficult keeping up. When she was at MGM, the studio never showed the contract players their fan mail. "If we knew how much we were getting," Ann said, "they were afraid we'd ask for more money." Ann giggled. "Sometimes I get letters from twelve-year-old boys asking if I'm married."

Chuckling, I helped Ann sit down on a loveseat beside the back door and handed her the bouquet. "Would you like me to put these in water for you?"

"No!" she said, clutching them tighter. "I want to hold them." She looked down at the flowers. "They *happy* me."

A smile stretched clear across my face. "I love that expression."

"Well," Ann said, "if something can sadden you, why can't it happy you?"

"I'm going to start saying that, too. I'll give you credit."

"You don't have to. It's yours."

I sat down beside her, scanned the room, and let out my breath. "I can't believe I'm actually in the home of a movie star. I just want to soak it all up."

"You *soak*."

On a nearby table sat a thick white binder open to a glamorous headshot of Ann. I reached for it and set it on my lap. As I flipped through the plastic sleeves, I discovered that the album was stuffed with page after page of magazine covers from the '30s, '40s, and '50s: *Better Homes & Gardens, Movie Romances, Photoplay, Modern Screen, Movie Mirror, Look, Hollywood, True Story,* and *Movie Story.* Each one had Ann's picture on it.

Years earlier, Ann received a phone message from someone in Spartanburg, South Carolina. When she heard the message she thought, I haven't been to Spartanburg since Metro sent me to be Queen of the Cottonville Festival in 1939. Ann returned the call, and a man named Bob answered the phone. Bob said that his wife Frannie had been "collecting" Ann since she was thirteen. When Frannie saw Ann in the Cotton Parade, she turned to her mother and said, "I want to collect her!" So, Frannie's mom notified everyone in the family. "If you see anything in the papers about Ann Rutherford," she told them, "clip it out and send it to Frannie." Bob and Frannie were downsizing and wanted to know if Ann wanted the albums. Ann said she'd love to have them. Then Frannie got on the line. "She knew more about my life than I did!" Ann said. When she received the albums, Ann was stunned. They were full of things she'd never seen before.

One year, Frannie and Bob invited Ann out for a visit, and she accepted. Ann said she didn't do house guesting, so they put her up in a nice hotel. While Ann was there, Bob and Frannie had her over for tea. They invited their relatives and all the neighbors. The mayor of the city was there, too. He presented Ann with a flag and assured her that it had flown over the state capitol. "Well," Ann said to me with a chuckle, "I couldn't fly it. It was a Confederate flag." She turned to me. "You know any Confederates?"

I turned the page in the album to reveal a beautiful magazine cover from 1940. On it, Ann was wearing a pink dress and holding a parasol.

Ann adjusted her glasses and smiled at the cover. "They made that when *Pride and Prejudice* came out. That's one of my costumes in the picture."

"Look how stunning you are," I said.

"Well," she said, matter of factly, "when you're young, you look good."

Ann told me that since then the British have made several versions of *Pride and Prejudice*, some more historically accurate, but the Jane Austen Society informed her that the 1940 adaptation is the one they show to their new members. Ann seemed proud of that.

Just then the telephone rang. I got up and brought the phone over to Ann. "Hello," she said. "Ann Rutherford? I'm sorry. She's not here." And she hung up. Smiling, Ann shook her head at herself. "As I get older, I keep getting worse." Then she twitched me a grin. "I'm working on it." Ann looked back at the album. "Now where were we?"

"We were talking about *Pride and Prejudice*."

"Oh, yes. My greatest grief when I look at the picture today is that it was shot in black and white. The picture was supposed to be shot in color, but it was made at the same time as *Gone With the Wind* and *The Wizard of Oz*. At that time there were only seven or eight Technicolor cameras in existence. *The Wind* and *Oz* gobbled up every last inch of Technicolor film. There was nothing left. Metro had obligated itself to everyone in the cast and couldn't wait. So they were forced to shoot it in black and white."

The next couple of album pages showed Ann in a variety of advertisements: Cannon hosiery, Royal Crown Cola, Miracle Whip, Jergen's lotion. There was even one of Ann selling canaries. Sometimes, Ann's image was used without permission. She reached over and turned a few of the sleeves. "Here," she said, pointing. "This is one of my favorites." The advertisement was for Glover's hair medicine and proclaimed to "cure the mange." Ann hooted. "Don't you just love it," she said, laughing. "I'm a spokesperson for the mange!" Ann showed me another ad for which she hadn't given her approval. In it she was holding a glass of Schaefer Beer. The advertisement stated that Ann and her friends all agreed that it was the finest beer they'd ever tasted. Ann turned to me and said, "I never even tried it."

Eventually I came to several black-and-white stills of Ann in *Gone With the Wind*. I stopped at one where she was posed with her two sisters, played by Vivien Leigh and Evelyn Keyes, at the foot of the stairs at Twelve Oaks, the Wilkes's plantation. In the photo, her skirt and collar were trimmed with a large Grecian key pattern. She wore a small matching hat. Ann said it was her favorite costume in the picture.

"Do you have anything from *Gone With the Wind*?" I asked.

"No. Not anymore," she said. "I used to, but I've given it all away." Ann paused. "Wait. I might still have a *Gone With the Wind* candy box somewhere." *

"They made *Gone With the Wind* candy?"

"Yes. The cast members had candies named after them — Melanie Molasses and Prissy Peppermints. My picture was on the back of the box. I'll see if I can find it and show you." Ann set the flowers down beside her. "One afternoon I was cleaning out my garage with some workmen when they found a big old crate up in the crawl space and asked what it was. 'Hell, I don't know!' I said. The men carried it down the ladder and opened it up. Inside was a beautiful Wedgwood demitasse set for twelve with delicate cups and saucers. Each cup was painted with a different scene in Georgia. Back in the fifties, several of the cast members had attended a reunion for *The Wind*, and they'd gifted each of us this set. I believe it was for the hundredth anniversary of the founding of Atlanta, but I'm not exactly sure about that. Anyway, I had completely forgotten about it. Thank God for my mother. She'd packed it up. If it had been left up to me, I wouldn't have known what happened to it from the day I left Atlanta."

The corners of Ann's mouth rose. "There was another smaller box in the crate," she continued. "I opened it up, and inside were four Hardy scripts and one from *A Christmas Carol*." My eyes bugged. "I'd forgotten all about them. The crate was sent to me after my aunt died."

"How did your aunt get the scripts?"

"Well, once in a while after I tossed one out …"

---

* When *Gone With the Wind* was released, Loew's promoted Ann at every turn. The back of the "Scarlett Chocolates" box by Nunnally's in Atlanta featured a photo of "Carreen O'Hara." Ann was also featured in the film's pressbook modeling *Gone With the Wind* scarves. There were two sets of *Gone With the Wind* paper dolls. The 5-doll set included one of "Ann Rutherford as Carreen." She was also part of the 18-doll set.

"You threw them *out?*" I interrupted.

Ann gave me a look. "Do you keep your phone books? I had no idea they'd be valuable someday. No one did. Unbeknownst to me, my mother had pulled them out of the trash and sent them to my aunt to let her know what I was working on. My aunt saved them, and after she passed away they sent me the box." Then, with a Cheshire cat grin, Ann held up her index finger. "But … that's not *all* that was in the box," she almost sang. Ann waited a beat. "There was another manila envelope with my mother's handwriting on it. I opened it up and pulled out a stack of paper. My name was on the front page. As I stared at it, I thought — it has finally happened. My mind has gone. I'm looking at something that doesn't exist."

I grabbed Ann's arm. "What was it?"

"The first hundred or so pages of my script from *Gone With the Wind.*"

I let out a shout.

"As far as I knew," Ann said, "everyone else had thrown theirs away."

"Do you have it here?" I asked quickly.

"I gave it to a museum. The interesting thing is that many of the lines aren't like anything you eventually see in the movie. They were constantly making changes."

As I recovered, Ann leaned over the photo with the Grecian key costume and pointed to a heart-shaped locket around her neck. She smiled as if seeing an old friend.

"I loved that piece," Ann said.

"The necklace?"

"Yes. I was the maid of honor for my best friend up in San Francisco, and she gave me the locket as a gift. Her father was a jeweler. It was gold with a diamond in the center. I never took it off.

I wore it in all of my pictures. If I didn't wear it outside of my costume, I'd tuck it underneath. It was my good luck charm." Ann smiled broadly. "And it worked every day."

The Lace and the Locket

When I drove over to Selznick Studios to begin work on The Wind, I reported to the wardrobe department for a costume fitting. The room smelled of new cloth and hot irons and buzzed with men and women with measuring tapes around their necks and pins in their aprons. Everywhere costumers were cutting, piecing, sewing, pinning, and running fabric through loud, heavy-duty sewing machines. Dresses in all stages of production were lying on tables and draped over hoops with bustles. In one corner, milliners sewed beads on hats. In another, an elderly woman was stitching an antebellum corset. Scattered around the tables lay designs by Walter Plunkett, who had drawn thousands of sketches for the film. It was all wonderfully exciting.

MGM had already sent over my nelly. A nelly was an exact form of your body. I'm not sure why they called it that. I remember the day they made mine. It was quite an ordeal. I stood in Metro's wardrobe department with my arms out. A couple of women covered me with canvas and pinned every seam. Then they cut me out of it, put in a zipper, sewed it back up, and stuffed it with sawdust. When I first started at MGM, I assumed everyone had a nelly, but they didn't. It was an honor to have one. If an actor gained weight, they had to make a new one. It was a matter of personal pride not to "outgrow" one's nelly. I always had the same one.

In Gone With the Wind, *all the women wore corsets, pantaloons, hoops, and large skirts. Each of my costumes must have weighed at least twenty pounds. You can't imagine the ordeal it was just to use the ladies' room. As I stood there in Selznick Studios being fitted, I couldn't believe the amount of ruffles on my petticoats and pantalets. They were adorned with row upon row of colored ribbon and beautiful lace. What a waste, I thought. I wasn't in the napping scene at Twelve Oaks, where all the girls lie down upstairs with their dresses off. No one was going to see this lace. They could have made my undergarments out of muslin. I was also given expensive leather shoes with little buttons that ran up the side. Mr. Selznick had brought over a marvelous Italian boot maker from New York. But nobody was going to see those, either.*

After a while, I heard David's voice in the building. He was passing through. I decided — I'm going to help this man save some money.

"Mr. Selznick," I called out as he walked by, "may I speak with you for a second, please?" He came over, and I pulled up my skirt to reveal my undergarments, "See these petticoats? Now I've done westerns and pictures set in the Civil War, so I know how women dressed, but no one will even see all these ruffles."

He put his hand up and said, "You'll know."

"But ... "

"My dear," he said, cutting me off, "you are the daughter of one of the wealthiest plantation owners in the county. And that *is how he dresses his daughters. Now, stop your yacking and get back to your fitting."*

A week or so later, I reported to David's office to show him my costumes. At our final fittings, you had to present your costumes to him. He insisted on seeing every one. The room was decorated with chintz curtains and upholstered chairs. It looked more like a comfortable study in a home than an executive's office. David was sitting at a large desk, smoking a cigarette. Walter Plunkett stood against the wall.

I was wearing a plaid skirt with a blue velvet sash and a short matching vest — my opening costume in the picture. David asked me to stand at the door, walk toward him, then make a few turns. I stepped forward as he told me to. When I completed my spin, David looked at Mr. Plunkett and said, "I thought I told you not to accessorize anything yet."

"I didn't," Mr. Plunkett replied.

"Then what is that?*" David said, pointing.*

I reached up and touched the locket. I knew exactly what he was talking about.

David stubbed out his cigarette, got up, and approached me.

"I'm sorry," I said. "It's mine. I forgot to tuck it in."

"Oh," said David. He looked back at Mr. Plunkett, grinned apologetically, and started back to his desk.

"Well actually, Mr. Selznick," I said, "would it be OK if I wear it in the picture? It's very special to me." I turned to Mr. Plunkett. "Please?"

David walked back over and furrowed his eyebrows as he examined it. "Well …" he said, "… it looks like it could be from that period." He glanced over at Mr. Plunkett, who gave a nod of agreement. "Yes," David said, "you may wear it."

Ann wears her favorite costume with the Grecian key pattern in a wardrobe test for *Gone With the Wind*. Notice that she is wearing her locket and that "Carreen" is misspelled on the clapboard.

— photo courtesy of the Herb Bridges Collection

Ann poses as Carreen O'Hara in *Gone With the Wind* (1939). She referred
to the film as the "Mona Lisa of motion pictures."
— photo from the private collection of Ann Rutherford courtesy of
Marietta Gone With the Wind Museum

Evelyn Keyes, Alicia Rhett and Ann Rutherford on the set for *Gone With the Wind*. Alicia is drawing Ann's portrait. An artist, Rhett often drew portraits between scenes. Notice Ann's locket and the wheat in her hat.
— photo courtesy of the Herb Bridges Collection

A publicity still of Ann Rutherford, Vivien Leigh and Evelyn Keyes at
Twelve Oaks. Ann is wearing her locket.
— photo from the private collection of Miss Rutherford
courtesy of Marietta Gone With the Wind Museum

Ann Rutherford and Evelyn Keyes in the car at Selznick Studios during
filming of *Gone With the Wind*.
— photo courtesy of the Patrick Picking Collection

Ann twirls in front of Tara wearing her favorite Grecian key costume
in *Gone With the Wind.*
— photo from the private collection of Ann Rutherford courtesy of
Marietta Gone With the Wind Museum

The House

Have a very good reason for everything you do.
— *Laurence Olivier*

Years later, when Ann was going through her dresser drawer, she came across the locket. As she held it in her hand, she knew just what to do with it. She packed it up and sent it to her friend Chris Sullivan for his birthday. He had one of the largest *Gone With the Wind* collections in the country. When Chris opened the envelope, Ann said he just about fell over. He immediately knew what it was. Eventually he had the locket mounted. It's now on display at the Marietta museum beside a photo of Ann wearing it in the picture.

"And the nelly," I asked. "What happened to that?"

"I had it for years before giving it away to a fan." Ann snorted lightly as she answered. "It makes me laugh to think that somebody out there has a life-sized stuffed me."

At that moment, a tall, stocky man in his mid-twenties stepped into the room. He was the one who'd driven Ann home. "I'm going out shopping, Miss Rutherford," he said. "Do you need anything?"

Ann asked him to put the flowers in some water. When he left the room, she told me that his name was Victor. He looked after her. Victor's father had been Ann's chief groundskeeper for years. "I call him Junior," Ann said, snickering. "Here he is this strapping guy who could carry a tractor, and I call him *Junior*. I'm sure he's part genius. He never has to look at a manual. Once I got a new fax machine, and it looked like a locomotive to me. I fiddled with it for weeks, but just knew I'd never be able to make it work. Well, Junior took one look at it and pressed a few buttons. Then it started spewing out the dozens of faxes I'd received since I got it."

Recently Victor had driven Ann to a big Hollywood event at the Egyptian Theatre in Los Angeles. Ann was all decked out. Because her car was in the shop, she had to ride in Victor's old pick-up. Well, Ann refused to be seen in his beat-up jalopy. So, she had Victor drop her off a couple of blocks away from the theater, then follow slowly behind her to make sure she got there OK.

The phone rang again, and Ann picked it up. She smiled broadly as she chatted. After she hung up, she told me it had been Al, the man she was with when I first met her at the Roosevelt Hotel. Al, she said, phoned every morning to see how she was. Ann called him her living alarm clock.

Then Ann asked if I would like to see the house. I was hoping she would. Ann reached for her cane, and I helped her stand. With her arm locked in mine, we walked back through the sunroom into the entryway. Ann pointed out two delicately carved mahogany pieces on each side of the door. "Bet you can't guess what those are," she said. "They are real wig stands from the eighteenth century." We took a few more steps, and she gestured to a tall, wooden bucket with double handles. It was stuffed with canes and umbrellas. "And this is an old English piece of firefighting equipment. They didn't have hoses back then. Don't you just love it? I'm fascinated with using things not quite for their original purpose. It gives you something to think about, to talk about." Ann looked down at herself and shook her head. "I'm like that old bucket, I guess. What you see is not for its original purpose."

Ann led me over to the staircase where she touched one of the white railings. "See this?" she said, leaning in. Carved into each railing were three stalks of wheat. "Remember the dress with the Grecian key pattern?" Ann said. "Do you recall the hat I was wearing with it? It was decorated with wheat. No one else had wheat on her hat. When I moved into this house, I took it as a sign."

Our first stop was the powder room. On the wall directly in front of us hung a large portrait of Ann. She was wearing a pink dress with giant sleeves and holding a parasol.

"That's the magazine cover I saw in the album!" I said excitedly. "The one from *Pride and Prejudice*."

"Yes, the painter gave it to my mother."

As we looked up at the portrait, I asked Ann if she enjoyed making the film.

"Oh, yes," she said. "I was thrilled. It was one of the most joyous experiences of my life. I got to work with all those British character actors with those wonderful faces. And I loved playing Lydia. It was one of my favorite roles. I wasn't a goody-two-shoes. I got to run away without being married. When I made the picture, I hadn't realized what a key role it was. Lydia drives the story. If she hadn't run off without the benefit of clergy, there'd be no reason for Laurence Olivier to chase down that cad and rescue her. Oh, I just loved coming home with the bugles ringing and the servants in their secondhand finery." Ann started singing "Lydia, the Tattooed Lady" from The Marx Brothers' picture *At the Circus*. "Lydia, oh Lydia. Say have you met Lydia? She has eyes that folks adore so ..." Ann stopped. "I love the name. Even today, people ask me to sign things as Lydia."

When shooting *Pride and Prejudice*, Ann said it was always

springtime. The director, Bob Leonard, whom everyone called Pop, had a property man with a huge box of paper flowers, and wherever the five daughters went, everything bloomed. Pop was an old-time director: Do it the way that feels right; keep it pleasant. He pretty much turned the actresses loose at rehearsals. During filming, Ann said that the ham in her came out. Pop encouraged it. He didn't tell the actors what to do. He told them what he wanted the results to be. "That," Ann said, "is the difference between a good director and a *schmuck*."

Ann took a step toward the portrait. "Adrian was the most remarkable designer. He designed all the costumes for the picture. Every detail was exquisite. He wanted the women to wear the Empire gowns, which was true to the period. Wet nightgowns, we called them. But when Greer Garson took over the lead (it was originally planned for Norma Shearer), she didn't want to wear Empire. So, the costumes were redesigned with full skirts and leg-of-mutton sleeves.

"Once we started shooting, we ran into all sorts of problems with those bulging skirts. The studio had neglected to consult Cedric Gibbons about the costume change. He was head of the art department. Before making the picture, they'd sent designers to comb England for choice little bits of furniture."

"Like your wig stands."

"Yes. The buyers were thinking Empire — slender gowns, spindly furniture, little rooms, tiny fireplaces. But when they came home with all these treasured antiques, they saw ship-in-full-sail skirts and sleeves so big you had to turn into the door sideways."

Ann and I left the powder room and stepped into a large living room, where the tabletops were loaded with knickknacks and pieces of art. Impressionist paintings in thick, gilded frames hung over a yellow sofa. Above the windows, upholstered valances capped draperies that puddled on the shiny hardwood floors. Ann's home was decorated in the early '40s and again in the '50s by former MGM star William Haines who went on to became the preeminent decorator to many of Hollywood's elite, including Joan Crawford, L.B. Mayer, George Cukor, and Carole Lombard.

In the corner of the room, photographs in silver and gold frames covered the lid of a black grand piano. In one of the photos, Ann was standing with John F. Kennedy. It was taken in the forties at MGM. The two knew each other. Ann had dated his older brother Joe a few times. In 1963, just months before John was assassinated, Ann attended a formal dinner at the White House. The guests all sat at round tables. At each one stood an empty chair so that when the president made his rounds he had a place to sit. During dinner, Ann set the photo of the two of them face down in front of the empty chair. When President Kennedy came by, he sat down and turned the photo over. After a good laugh, he shook his head and said, "Was anybody ever that young?"

As Ann and I toured the room, she pointed out various objects she had collected from her travels. On one table sat a delicate porcelain cupid surrounded by pastel garlands. With shaky hands, she picked it up, then turned it over to show me the double cross Meissen mark underneath. The piece, Ann said, was supposed to be in *Pride and Prejudice.* On the first day of shooting, all five sisters and their mother were scuttling around the room in their wide hoop skirts, and everything was falling over. Suddenly Ann heard a clink. She looked over and saw the porcelain cupid lying on the floor in two pieces. Quickly the prop man came over, picked up the broken pieces, and to Ann's dismay, threw them into the garbage. No effort was made to salvage it. When they called a coffee break, Ann sneaked over to the trash barrel, leaned into it with her giant hoops sticking out and her petticoats showing, and grabbed the broken pieces. Then she went over to the prop man and asked if he had any glue. He gave her some, and Ann went back to her dressing room and put it back together.

Back then, Ann said, the studios had money to burn. It was an era when money was no object. Costumes were made with the finest silks and velvets. Milliners and embroiderers were brought over from Europe. Ann recalled one day on the set of *Pride and Prejudice* when Olivier was sitting at an antique desk. It was a little too high for the cameraman. Rather than adjust the height of the camera, someone called out, "Get the carpenter!" He came and chopped a few inches off the legs.

Ann gasped when I asked about working with Laurence Olivier. "It was like oiled silk," she said. "I'd fallen in love with him when I saw *Wuthering Heights*. A date took me to see the picture. After he brought me home, I sat in the living room just thinking about Olivier with those half-masked eyes. Pretty soon, my mother came down the stairs. 'Why aren't you in bed?' she asked. 'I can't,' I cried. 'I'm still thinking of *Wuthering Heights*.' He blew my mind." Ann turned to me. "You know the scene when he is carrying Merle Oberon? I started crying then." She paused. "I think I'm still cryin'.

"And then," Ann continued, "imagine how I felt when I found out that I was going to *work* with him. He was so beautiful. I think I spent most of my time closing my mouth. When I first met him, I could barely get two words out. And he didn't call me Miss Rutherford. At that time we all called each other by our last names. He called me by Ann! Oh, my cup runneth over. It leaked. It filled the whole house.

"I didn't have any scenes directly with him, but I watched him and listened. And when he had all those scenes with Greer Garson, my jaw was open, tongue extended. The banter between those two. Back and forth and back and forth, like a table tennis match. My God! I could sit and watch that picture over and over just to see the two of them."

As Ann and I returned to the entry, she said that during breaks Olivier would study his script for *Romeo and Juliet*. He and Vivien Leigh were preparing to take it to Broadway. In *Pride and Prejudice*, Olivier wore a false nose. He was breaking it in for the part of Romeo. Ann said the makeup people had a heck of a time trying to make sure the seams didn't show. Ann also told me that all the money Olivier made from *Wuthering Heights* and Leigh earned from *Gone With the Wind* went into the ill-fated *Romeo and Juliet*. "They lost everything," Ann said.

Next, Ann and I stepped into the library, where French doors looked out into the grand backyard and hundreds of books, many inscribed to her by their authors, squeezed between bookends on floor-to-ceiling shelves. Ann was an avid reader. When shooting *Pride and Prejudice*, she became a big fan of Jane Austen's works. Before that, her favorite author had been Charles Dickens. When Ann was young, parts of an unpublished Dickens manuscript were discovered, and the *Los Angeles Evening Herald* published it in installments. For months, Ann saved it until she had the whole book.

Ann in her favorite role as Lydia in *Pride and Prejudice* (1940)
— photo courtesy of the Christopher P. Sullivan Collection

Ann Rutherford in *Pride and Prejudice* (1940).
The portrait of Ann that hung in her house was painted from this
photograph.
— photo courtesy of the Patrick Picking Collection

Ann checks her makeup while a hairdresser attends to her hair ribbon for
Pride and Prejudice (1940). The photo was taken on location in Pasadena's
Busch Gardens.
— photo courtesy of the James Bawden Collection

As we walked through the library, Ann pointed out a table in the corner of the room where David Selznick liked to play cards. Tucked off the library stood the bar with a vinyl booth like you'd see in a '40s diner. Behind the counter, glass shelves full of tumblers and bottles laddered up a mirrored wall. Ann said the bar used to be the favorite room in the house.

When we returned to the sunroom where we'd started, I helped Ann sit down and asked if I could look outside. In the backyard, tall palm trees shaded lush flowerbeds with hibiscus and birds of paradise. I walked around the pool to a large side yard where the workman who'd called Ann for me was carrying some Sheetrock. I stepped back inside and asked what he was working on. Ann said he was repairing the maid's quarters.

In the '60s, Ann's second husband, Bill Dozier, and she brought over a couple from Hong Kong named Ah Ying and Ah Cha. Ah Ying was the maid, and her husband Ah Cha was the cook. Betsy Bloomingdale had recommended them; they were her cook's friends. It took Ann and Bill a year to get the two over to the States because they had to prove they had talents that couldn't be found elsewhere. Ah Ying and Ah Cha lived in the maid's quarters. They had four children. Two came with them, and two stayed in Hong Kong. At the end of their first year with Ann and Bill, Ah Cha said he wanted to bring over his other two children. When Ann asked him why he didn't bring them when they first came, he said, "Not sure we want."

Ah Ying, Ann recalled, was like a court maid from the days of Napoleon. She stuffed the sleeves of Ann's dresses with tissue paper, which made getting dressed quite a noisy affair, and ironed Ann's panty hose so that they looked like they just came out of the package. One day, Ann noticed that her husband's underpants had started to come undone. She started ripping them apart, then put them in a drawer. A couple of days later, Bill walked into the bedroom holding up the underpants and said, "I hope I'm in an accident." Ann asked why. "Because," Bill said, "when they undress me in the hospital, they'll see that someone liked me enough to embroider my underpants." Ah Ying had embroidered his briefs.

Ah Cha was a magician in the kitchen. "He could cook anything in any language," Ann said. Sometimes he prepared something so thin that you couldn't see it on the pan. He even kept a bicycle pump in the pantry that he used to puff the skin off a duck. Ah Cha cooked all the meals except for the big parties, which they had catered.

Ann and Bill were known for their parties. In those days, the trend was to cover the entire yard with a tent. They used to have the pool covered with a dance floor, and the band played at the pool house. Their big party was on Groundhog Day. All the other holidays were taken, and they didn't want to give a party when everyone else did. Their philosophy was that in order for a party to be good, you have to celebrate something. So, they celebrated Groundhog Day. But they didn't have it every year. They held it every other year so it wouldn't become redundant.

"Who came to your parties?" I asked.

"Oh, just about everyone in my address book," Ann replied. "Debbie Reynolds and Eddie Fisher. Donna Reed and her husband came. Edward G. Robinson and Harold Lloyd. He used to shake with his left hand after he lost part of his right one in an accident. Louella Parsons, the Hollywood columnist, and her husband Henry Martin came. Marilyn Monroe ..."

My eyes widened. "Marilyn Monroe was in this house?"

"Many times."

Since Bill was a studio executive, he had to watch the dailies every evening. Bill and Ann had a theater built out back so that Bill could watch them at home. It had since burned down. Ann had decorated it in an Asian motif. It had about twenty seats and sliding glass doors that were very new back then. People kept running into them. After supper, Bill would go out to the theater. Often, other people came over to watch with him. Johnny Hyde, Marilyn Monroe's agent, used to bring Marilyn. "Johnny would park her out in the empty theater," Ann said. "She wouldn't even come ask for a drink. Bill would ask me to go out and keep her company. So, I'd bring her a Coke and sit with her. Believe it or not, we actually attended the same junior high. Marilyn loved watching the movies. Nobody bothered her there."

One Christmas, Ann had a slot car track built for Bill in the theater. It was on a large board about the size of four dining room tables put together. There were tracks and little cars. When the picture was over, they'd move away all the chairs, flick a switch, and the giant board would make its stately descent. "The guys couldn't wait to play," Ann said. "Marilyn loved to play, too."

Then Ann leaned over to me and whispered as if we weren't the only two in the room. "You know, Johnny Hyde had Marilyn ... *rearranged* a little." Ann paused. "Corrections were made." Ann tapped her nose and her chin to show me where. "It's all out in the open now, but no one knew at the time. In the fifties, that kind of thing was very new in Hollywood. But my husband knew."

I looked around the room, trying to imagine the celebrities that had been in Ann's home. I pictured women in cocktail hats and men wearing wing-tipped shoes. From where I was sitting, I could see into the "favorite room in the house." Who stood there? I thought. What were their favorite drinks? I looked outside and wondered who danced over the pool. Oh, what I would have given to be a fly on the wall in that house. I thought of other MGM stars Ann would have invited over.

"Was Gene Kelly ever here?" I asked.

"Yes," Ann said, nodding.

"Fred Astaire?"

"Yes."

"Joan Crawford?"

Ann didn't respond.

"Was Joan Crawford here?" I repeated.

Ann straightened. "She *wasn't* invited."

The Dinner Party

J *oan lived in a big house in Brentwood. It was a beautiful home with lots of rooms, a big fireplace, and silver in the cabinets. There was a grand swimming pool in the back. Joan's children and mine took piano lessons from the same teacher. Mrs. Schwinger was her name. The recitals used to be at Joan's home. She had a room with a small stage.*

One evening, Joan gave a dinner party. Soon after the guests arrived, she said, "Have you seen the twins?" She had just adopted twin babies. Joan had already adopted two others, a boy and a girl — the one who wrote Mommie Dearest, *which by the way I'm glad she wrote.*

Joan led us all upstairs, opened the door to the nursery, and flicked on the lights. The babies were asleep in their cribs. Then she woke each one and picked them up for us to see. I was appalled. These two little angels had been sound asleep. You don't do that to your dogs!

Later, we were all sitting around the dining table having dessert when her oldest son Christopher came into the room to say good night. He stepped over to his mother and said, "Good night, Mommie Dearest. I love you, Mommie Dearest." She really had them trained to say that. I felt so sorry for the child. After Christopher kissed his mother, he started walking out.

Just as he was at the end of the room, Joan called out to him. "Christopher!" He turned around. And then she announced, "Darling, have you gone tinkle?" Her son's face froze. Then he nodded quickly and ran upstairs. I was horrified. I felt so terrible for the little boy. Here he was old enough to be embarrassed, and she humiliated him. After the way she woke up her new twins and now this — I had had enough. I politely excused myself from the table.

A while later, Joan spotted me stepping out of the powder room. "Oh, there you are, darling," she intoned, in her la-di-da sort of way. "I've been looking for you. We didn't know where you were."

I straightened my back. "You embarrassed your child."

"Wh-what?" she said, flustered. "What are you talking about?"

"You heard me," I said. "At the dinner table. You asked your son if he had tinkled. You embarrassed him." Joan opened her mouth to speak, but I wouldn't let her. I looked her straight in the eye and said, "I have an adopted child myself. And do you know what I am going to do? I am going to go home right now, get on my knees, and thank God she didn't end up in your home."

Husbands and Show People

I'd marry again if I found a man who had fifteen million dollars, would sign over half to me, and guarantee that he'd be dead within a year.

— *Bette Davis*

"I couldn't abide her," Ann said, shaking her head. "I remember when Joan's daughter Christina came over to my house for my daughter's party. We had a seal, a pony, and Bozo the Clown. All the kids were out back playing in the pool and having a great old time. But not Christina. The poor girl had to sit on a patio chair in her white dress and gloves with her back straight and her hands folded in her lap. I felt so badly for her. When she wrote *Mommie Dearest*, Christina should have called me. I would have given her more stories."

As the afternoon passed into early evening, Ann shared story after story. She told me about the day when Howard Strickling, head of publicity at MGM, received a call from The May Company Department Store to ask if someone from the studio would narrate a fashion show. Howard asked Ann and she happily agreed. Ann lived close by. On the day of the show, hundreds of gloved women sat on each side of a long, red carpet. Since it was wartime, most of the women had lines drawn on the back of their legs to look like they were wearing stockings, which were scarce. Tom May Sr., the owner of the store, beamed from the corner of the room. Ann stood behind a podium wearing a tailored gray silk suit with an orchid pinned to her lapel. She knew that she probably shouldn't have worn that outfit to a May Company event. She'd bought it at Bloomingdale's.

As the models paraded down the runway, Ann enjoyed describing the clothes. She didn't use a script; with her gift of gab, she didn't need one. Because women needed to be industrious during the war, when a model walked out in a long dress, Ann explained that after wearing it a couple of times, they could cut off the bottom to make a skirt, or a turban, or have someone do them up a hat. Mr. May listened on, shocked. After the show, he went up to Ann and said he wished she hadn't suggested cutting up his clothes. To get him off the subject, Ann brought up his son. "Isn't your son Fred May?" She knew good and well that it was David. Tom started talking about David, and Ann was off the hook.

The next day Ann received a phone call from Tom's son, David May II. He had already spoken with Ann's mother. David asked Ann how she liked the store. Ann said it was lovely and that she shopped there a lot, but it wasn't always successful. She told him that she had recently bought some expensive gloves there, but they made a mark on the table. The next day, she received twelve pairs of gloves on her doorstep. They did not leave a mark.

It wasn't long until David asked Ann out, and the handsome couple could be seen dining at restaurants like La Rue, attending concerts at the Hollywood Bowl, or dancing at the Trocadero, where photographers would snap their photos for the movie magazines that followed the courtship and speculated on their engagement. On December 26, 1942, Ann and David were married at Tom and Anita

May's home in Beverly Hills. David presented Ann with a five-carat diamond ring. The guest list included many of Ann's studio colleagues: Laraine Day, Virginia O'Brien, Maureen O'Hara, Jackie Cooper, Anne Shirley, Robert Stack, and Deanna Durbin, whom everyone called Edna May. Louella Parsons arrived late and had to stand outside during the service. Gus, the butler, wouldn't let her in until after the ceremony.

Ann and David bought a ranch in Northridge, in the northwest corner of the San Fernando Valley. It had previously belonged to Barbara Stanwyck and Robert Taylor, who Ann described as prettier than any of the women. At that time, the valley was all citrus groves, alfalfa fields, acres of walnut and apricot trees, and horse ranches. There were only a few estates in the area. The first time Ann met Stanwyck, she was nervous. "I thought she'd be a *toughy*," Ann said. "In her pictures, she was often shooting people."

The following year, Ann and David moved to Beverly Hills. Ann had always wanted to live there. David bought one of the few available lots on Greenway Drive. About once a month, he flew to New York for business and considered it a lost trip if he didn't return with "something pretty" for Ann from Tiffany and Co. or Van Cleef & Arpels. "But that was OK by me," Ann sang, happily. "Spoil away!"

In 1944, Ann and David adopted their daughter Gloria when she was one day old. For a year, they kept the child a secret, and whenever anyone came over, they'd whisk the baby upstairs. The newlyweds were afraid that if the natural mother found out that the child's parents were well off, she'd make trouble.

Because the May Company was one of the largest retailers in the country, Ann was never in want for anything during the lean war years. Once, actress Gloria de Haven's mother called Ann in a panic to ask if she could borrow some stockings for her daughter's wedding. Ann had plenty, so she gave her a pair. From then on, Gloria always told everyone that she got married in Ann Rutherford's stockings. When Ann finished telling me the story, she took the wallet out of her handbag and pulled out a plastic card. Grinning, she held it up for me to see. It was the May Company employee discount card. She still had it.

During World War II, the studio put out movies as fast as they could to entertain the boys away from home and cheer up the wives and mothers who missed them. "I'd finish one picture at noon," Ann recalled, "then start another one after lunch."

When Ann heard that the U.S.S. *Arizona* sank during the attack on Pearl Harbor, it was an especially sobering moment. "The *Arizona* saved my life," Ann told me. When she was fourteen, her friends down the street made a boat. The teens took it to the Los Angeles harbor and set sail in the direction of Catalina. Ann went along. She made chicken sandwiches for the voyage. When they were well beyond the harbor, the boat started to leak. The caulk hadn't completely dried. As they scooped out buckets of water, Ann stood up, the boom hit her, and she fell overboard. Kicking furiously, Ann shouted that she couldn't swim! As her friends tried to help her back into the boat, it tipped over, and they fell in, too. "I watched the sandwiches wrapped in their waxed paper sink into the ocean," Ann remembered. "Here I'd just been thrown into the ocean and I was wondering what would happen to our lunch!"

Clinging to the overturned boat, Ann and her friends saw a ship on the horizon. It turned out to be the *Arizona*. Fortunately, a sailor spotted the capsized boat, and the ship sent a cutter out to rescue them. On the *Arizona*'s deck, they were given blankets and tea. That day said a lot about Ann's character. She wasn't going to go down without a fight. When she finished telling me the story, I said she should have accepted the offer to play Rose in *Titanic*. She had the experience.

Like many Hollywood stars, Ann did her part for the war effort. She went out on USO tours and danced the Jitterbug with the servicemen at the Hollywood Canteen. Her husband didn't mind. Metro sent Ann out on war bond drives with actor Charles Laughton. Ann said it was an odd pairing, but the audiences enjoyed them. The studio paid for the car and the driver. Ann's mother went along, too. Ann and Charles visited factories, linen houses, "anyplace where there were a couple of hundred people, anyplace we could get anybody with fifty cents." Charles recited old English poetry and verse, and Ann followed, taking questions from the audience. "I loved selling things," she said. As they'd drive from town to town, if Charles saw that they were nearing the ocean or a lake, he would get his feet out of his shoes and ask the driver to stop. Then he'd roll up his pant legs and wade in the water.

"It was like traveling with a willful nine-year-old kid on my heels," Ann recalled. "And I was like his mother. Charlie never had the least idea what he put into his suitcase and he was always leaving things behind. Whenever we arrived at a new hotel, he'd send me out to buy new socks or shirts or a toothbrush. The only thing he knew about packing was to grab a few things, stuff them into his suitcase, and sit on it." The team set a wartime fund-raising record. It hit the trade papers, and Ann was happy about that.

Ann and David's marriage ended after nine years. David wanted Ann to stop making pictures, and Ann said forget it. The divorce was amicable. In the settlement, Ann got life tenancy of the house. After their divorce, David came over regularly to pick up their daughter Gloria for visits, but Gloria would cry when she had to leave the nanny. When David would drop Gloria off, she'd cry again when she had to leave her daddy. These scenes were too much for Ann, so she insisted that David be at the house every day when Gloria went to school and again when she came home. Ann fixed up a study upstairs for David.

While they were still married, Ann and David used to have Joan Fontaine and her then-husband Bill Dozier over for dinner. At the time, Bill was head of the literary department at Paramount. He and Joan had a daughter named Deborah. After Bill and Joan divorced, Ann began seeing Bill. One evening, not long after the two started going out, Ann arrived late to a dinner party. Bill, a maniac about punctuality, grabbed a dictionary off the bookshelf, flipped through the pages, and ripped one out. He circled a single word with a pen, then handed the paper to Ann. The word was *telephone*. "You've heard of that, haven't you?" Bill said. "Well," Ann said to me, "I figured that any man who'd ruin a perfectly good unabridged dictionary must really care."

In 1953, Bill had to move to New York. At that time he was head of West Coast productions for CBS. He and Ann were not married yet. Ann and Gloria moved to New York to be near him. When I told Ann that I never knew she lived in New York, she responded, "I didn't either." Ann hadn't planned on it. She didn't rent out her house or even clean out a closet. She just closed the doors and left the dogs with the housekeeper.

In New York, Ann first lived at Eightieth and Park, but Gloria didn't like it because it was too far from the zoo. The cat also kept going out the window, and Ann was afraid it would fall forty floors. So they moved to Eighty-first and Fifth. Bill lived four blocks away with his daughter, Deborah, and Francis, the governess, who was the wife of Charlie Chaplain's valet.

The early '50s were Broadway's golden era, and Ann and Bill went to the theater as often as they could. They attended openings of the revivals of *Oklahoma!, Carousel,* and *Porgy and Bess,* as well as new shows, including *Kismet, Guys and Dolls, Damn Yankees,* and *Peter Pan.* Ann was proud of the fact that she'd flown before Mary Martin did in *Peter Pan.* Ann flew in MGM's *A Christmas Carol* as the Ghost of Christmas Past. The studio had never flown anyone before. To prepare her for flying, Ann lay on a table covered with plaster of Paris. After it dried, they cut everything away except the shelf and hid it under Ann's gown. "You can see it in the picture," Ann said. "It looks like I'm flying on an ironing board." One day, Ann was suspended in the air when the counterweight broke, and she snapped up to the ceiling. They had to call the fire department to get her down. Ann was fine, but said it scared the living daylights out of her. As for *A Christmas Carol,* Ann said she still received letters from people who run it every December. "It's become a holiday tradition," Ann said. "That's another picture that has legs."

Ann enjoyed telling a backstage story about her stepdaughter Deborah who, then in first grade, was in New York with her mother, Joan Fontaine. Fontaine was performing *Tea and Sympathy,* directed by Elia Kazan. Tony Perkins was also in the show. Deborah used to hang out backstage and watch the performers. In one of Tony's scenes, he pretended to have a bloody nose by holding it and lying on the floor. After the show, little Deborah walked up to him and said, "That's not how you stop a nosebleed." She showed him how, and Tony changed it. Ann chuckled at the memory. "Here's this big Broadway production directed by Elia Kazan, and a five-year-old is changing his direction."

In New York, it was Ann's daughter Gloria who proposed to Bill. "When are you going to marry my mother?" Gloria asked Bill one day. She gave Bill her ninth birthday to get married on. So that's the day Bill and Ann were married. They wed on October 5, 1953. The papers reported that Ann got married bareheaded after leaving her veiled cocktail hat in the taxi on the way to the ceremony.

In return for Gloria giving up her birthday, Ann knew she had to throw her daughter a special party and went crazy thinking of what to do. When Ann saw that Gene Autry was coming to town, she decided to take Gloria and her friends to see him. Ann would invite all the little girls in her class and their nannies, too. Gloria attended a private girls school. But when Ann called to get tickets, she struck out. She could not for the life of her get a block of them. Ann was beside herself. Then she thought — what am I *doing*? I'll just phone Gene! So, she called up her first leading man and explained the situation. He said, "Honey, how many rows do you want?" They ended up having terrific seats, and at the intermission, Gene invited the whole lot of them backstage. All the kids and their nannies crowded into his dressing room, and Gene let them sit on his saddle and try on his hat.

After Ann and Bill were married, they would set David May up on blind dates. Ann didn't want him to be alone. David and Bill affectionately referred to one another as their "husbands-in-law." Ann and Bill spent every Christmas Eve at the Mays' home. Ann continued to wear David's ring even when married to Bill. She said it made Bill look good. Bill and Joan Fontaine, however, did not remain on friendly terms. When Fontaine wrote her autobiography *No Bed of Roses*, she sent a signed copy to Bill. Furious, he scribbled, "Not one ounce of truth!" below her signature and sent it back.

In the 1960s, Bill produced the hit television series *Batman*. When preparing to produce the show, Bill asked his secretary to get everything she could find about the comic strip, and she jammed about thirty comic books into his suitcase. Bill had never read any of the comics. When Ann and Bill were on a plane to New York, Bill pulled them out and started reading. The steward came down the aisle and looked at Ann with an expression that said — you poor soul. I'm so sorry you're stuck with this clown reading *Batman.* When Bill started production, he interviewed lots of men for the famous voiceover that announces, "Tune in next week. Same Bat-time, same Bat-channel," but he wasn't pleased with any of the readings. Finally, the recording engineer said, "Why don't you just read the damn thing yourself." And he did. So, Bill was on every episode. He had to get his union card to do it. Bill asked Ann to be in *Batman,* but she said she wouldn't dream of it. She was having more fun with her children. "I was living my life backwards — *bass ackwards,*" Ann giggled. "You see, I started working too young. When I had my own kids, I was able to enjoy my second childhood."

Bill and Ann owned a beach house in Malibu right on the Pacific Coast Highway. From Greenway Drive, it was fourteen minutes door-to-door. They called it Greenway by the Sea. Ann loved it because her kitchen looked out over the ocean. She'd cook and make the salads, and Bill did all the barbecuing. They had an upstairs apartment that they rented to Mary Tyler Moore and her husband Grant Tinker.

At the beach house, Ann went through stages of redoing furniture. She taught Mary how to restore and sand, too. "I'm inclined to go overboard on something," Ann admitted with a smirk. Once when she was out driving, Ann spotted a truck loaded with little chairs. They were the same ones she remembered having at dance class when she was a little girl. Ann followed that truck for miles. Finally, when the driver stopped, Ann got out of her car and called out, "How much do you want for all those chairs?" The man asked why, and

Ann said, "I think I need them."

"How many chairs were there?" I asked Ann.

She made a face. "About fifty."

There seemed to be no end to Ann's friends. "If I had a problem with my pool," Ann said with a laugh, "I'd just phone Esther Williams. I figured of all people, *she'd* know how to fix a pool." Ann called Danny Kaye, with whom she filmed *The Secret Life of Walter Mitty*, the best cook in the world. He learned his lines while cooking. Peter Lawford and Ann were also close. Ann said that after Lawford "so cunningly" married a relative of the president, his mother and father became more regal than the queen. "They did everything but bless your hands and ask you to kiss them." Friend June Allyson was one of the best criers on the lot. Ann called her the Town Crier.

Debbie Reynolds lived just down the street. Once during a party at Ann's house, Debbie lost her wedding ring. She'd taken it off to wash her hands at the kitchen sink, and the next thing she knew it was in the garbage disposal. They had to call a plumber at two in the morning. When Eddie Fisher left Debbie for Elizabeth Taylor, Ann said it was madness on the block. The reporters practically camped out on Debbie's lawn. She couldn't go outdoors without them swarming her.

At one point in our conversation, Ann took me over to a framed picture on the wall. It was an editorial cartoon from the *New York Times* after Rosemary Clooney's death. In it, God's finger was pointing out of the clouds to Rosemary. He was saying, "Come on-a my house." Rosemary had been one of Ann's closest friends. The two met at the Biltmore Hotel in Vermont when Ann and David were on their honeymoon. One afternoon, Ann saw Rosemary sitting in the hotel lobby edging a piece of paper with paper clips. She walked over to Rosie, introduced herself, and said she just had to ask what Rosemary was doing. Rosemary said she was a reader for a men's magazine. The guy she worked for made so little money that he couldn't afford new paper clips, so she saved them.

When Bill had to go to New York for CBS, he asked Ann if she'd rent his place out for him. Ann rented it to Rosie with "everything down to the firewood." The house wasn't far from Ann's. Years later, George Clooney, Rosemary's nephew, was always showing up at Aunt Rosemary's. He'd climb over the wall, and Rosemary would call out, "Oh, shit. The kid's here again." Ann said George Clooney could well be our next Clark Gable.

Bonita Granville, whom Ann called Bonnie, had been Ann's best friend. Ann was the matron of honor at her wedding to Jack Rather and threw two baby showers for their children. At one time, Rather owned the *Queen Mary*, and Ann and Bonita would spend hours exploring the ship. When Disneyland opened, Jack and Bonita invited Ann to join them for the opening ceremonies. Jack had built the Disneyland Hotel. He named the restaurant Granville Steak House and one of the wings the Bonita Tower. At some time during the festivities, Ann was heading into the hotel's gift shop when she ran into Walt Disney. "What are you up for today, Ann?" Walt asked her. They'd met the day before. "I'm going to buy a Mickey Mouse," said Ann. Walt put up his hands and said, "Hold the boat." Then he dashed into the shop and came out with a stuffed Mickey.

"You have a Mickey Mouse from Walt Disney?" I asked, surprised.

"Yes," Ann answered. "I was shocked that he didn't even buy it."

I smiled. "Uh ... I don't think he had to." Then I shook my head. "Ann, you knew *everybody*."

"I think I did," she replied with a shrug. "It was a friendly world back then. And a very small one. If you worked at the same studio, you were a big brother or a little sister to anyone else on the lot. We saw each other every day. We were family. If you didn't work at the same studio, you recognized one another, or had seen something they were in, or hated something they had done. If that was the case, you'd just say, 'I *saw* you!'

"I'm so blessed to have known so many remarkable people," Ann continued. "When you're young, you just take these things for granted. It never occurred to us to collect autographs from anyone. The only ones who collected them were children. And none of us dreamed of asking each other for a photo. Next time you come ..." That made me smile. "... I'll dig out my photographs, and we can look at them."

"I'd love that." I looked out the window. It was starting to get dark. Then I glanced at my watch. "Yikes," I said. "Do you realize how long we've been talking? Five hours!"

"Oh, my," she said. "And I never even offered you anything to eat. I'm so sorry."

"No problem," I said. "But I better get going."

Ann and I made plans to meet two days later. I'd pick her up on Wednesday for our lunch date at the Polo Lounge. I gave her a kiss good-bye and told her not to get up, but she insisted on walking with me to the door anyway. As we stepped onto the front porch, Ann looked out at my rental car and asked what kind it was. I told her it was a Ford, and she approved.

On the way back to Santa Monica, I stopped at the store, grabbed some dinner, then drove to my friend Paul's place. When Paul got home from work, I told him all about my visit with Ann. Paul was an actor and a screenwriter. He loved hearing the stories.

"You know why she invited you to come out here, don't you?" Paul said. "She wants you to write her book."

"No, she doesn't," I said, pulling a face.

"Of course she does. Why else would she be talking with you? Think about it. A famous old movie star discovers a young writer …" Paul smiled. "OK — a not so young writer — who is as passionate about old Hollywood as she is. I think it's pretty clear."

I shook my head. "She told me she didn't want to write a book."

"When?"

"A couple of years ago."

"She's changed her mind. Listen, Phil. From what you've told me, this woman has devoted a great deal of her life sharing stories about her career. Why? Because it's important to her. Ann knows she's not going to be around forever." Paul pointed at me. "She wants *you* to write her book, Mr. Done."

"But she didn't say anything."

"She's saying plenty. How many hours did you just spend with her today?"

I hesitated. "… five."

"*Five* hours?" Paul stepped into the kitchen and called out, "How many writers do you know who get to sit with a movie star for five hours? You don't see it Phil, but it's just like Willie Wonka."

"*Huh?*"

"Willie Wonka knew he wasn't going to last forever, so what does he do? He calls five kids to his chocolate factory in hopes of finding someone to take over, to carry on his vision. He picks a boy named Charlie Bucket." Paul poked his head from around the corner. "*You*, my friend, are Ann Rutherford's Charlie Bucket."

Ann Rutherford and Bill Dozier attend the premiere of *The Hasty Heart* at a Hollywood theater (1949).
— photo courtesy of the private collection of Miss Rutherford

Ann Rutherford and Bonita Granville (1942). The caption on the back
reads, "Ann Rutherford and Bonita Granville, two of Metro-Goldwyn
Mayer's young starlets, took time off from their picture chores to prove
their prowess at bowling. They rate as tops in the Hollywood's youngest at
the sport which is now sweeping the movie colony."
— photo courtesy of the James Bawden Collection

Ann prepares for a wedding shower in her dining room in the early '40s.
— photo courtesy of the James Bawden Collection

Ann and her friends sewing at her Beverly Hills home in 1945. From left to right: Frances Rafferty, Ann Miller, Mrs. Bob Hutton, Betty Newling, Ann Rutherford and Bonita Granville.
— photo courtesy of the James Bawden Collection

Ann Rutherford on a war bond tour. On Sept. 8, 1942, *The Film Daily* reported, "For the New York area, Charles Laughton, Virginia Grey, and Ann Rutherford continued their smashing success of millions in bond sales in the metropolitan area with equally large sales in Connecticut."
— photo courtesy of the private collection of Miss Rutherford

Ann Rutherford sits at a party at her home at Greenway Drive (1956). On her right is director Fred Cordova. Ann's daughter Gloria is kneeling.
— photo courtesy of the James Bawden Collection

The Polo Lounge

There are only two kinds of class — first class and no class.
— *David O. Selznick*

That night I thought a lot about what Paul said. Of course I'd love to write Ann's biography. It would be a thrill to write it. But I didn't agree with him. If Ann wanted me to write her memoir, she would have asked. The reason she invited me to Beverly Hills was because she genuinely loved people. She loved life. She once told me, "I don't know anyone who's been on this earth twice, so I'm going to live it up to the fullest." Ann knew that fans like me were incredibly interested in her life, so she shared it freely. What had she called it? Gracious living. *That's* the reason she invited me to her home. She was living graciously. I was sure of it.

Wednesday was the big day — our trip to the Polo Lounge. Again, it was a beautiful California afternoon. No clouds. The sky — Tiffany box blue. When I stepped out of the car, I could hear carpenters working on the maid's quarters. As I walked up to the house, I dodged the spray of the automatic sprinklers that were watering the roses. The front door was open, and I could see Ann's silhouette on a chair in the sunroom. She was waiting for me.

"*Helloooo,*" I announced, stepping inside.

"Is that you, Phil?" Ann called out.

"Yes."

Ann was dressed in a sharp turquoise pantsuit. She'd put on lipstick and rouge. On her lapel, she wore a large, diamond-encrusted butterfly pin that only a movie star or a princess could get away with. She also wore the diamond ring from David May.

"You look lovely," I said.

"Why thank you," she said, smiling. "Scarlett would want her little sister looking nice." I laughed as she handed me her cane. "You know why I carry a clear cane?" she asked. "It matches everything I own."

As I helped her up, Ann said she was going to kill the workmen. "This morning, they turned off the water! It just came back on. So, I made a speech. 'It is a given,' I said, 'that you notify the occupant before you turn off the goddamned water!' "

Arms connected, Ann and I walked outside, and she locked the door. She dropped the key into her purse and announced, "Key, you're in my handbag." She turned to me. "If I say it out loud, I'm less apt to forget where I put it. It sort of indents it." Then Ann sighed. "Honey, I have reached a point in my life where I can't find anything. I couldn't find my fanny with both hands."

This woman's a riot.

When we reached the driveway, Ann called out, "Don't forget to feed the cat!"

"You have a cat?"

Ann dropped her voice. "No. I always say that when I leave. That way, any burglars lurking in the bushes will think someone is at home."

As we drove out the driveway, Ann pointed to the golf course across the street. Before they changed the hole, her lawn used to be covered with golf balls. Some mornings when she went outside to get her morning paper, it looked like she was having an Easter egg hunt. If a ball had a mark on it, it went back over the fence. If it was pure and perfect, she'd put it in an egg carton and bring it to her dentist. Once in a while, she still found a golf ball on the lawn.

The Beverly Hills Hotel was just a few blocks away. On the way, Ann pointed to the divider in the center of the road and explained that in the old days it had been a riding track. People could rent a horse behind the hotel and gallop a trot.

"Now, Phil," Ann said, "in order to get my favorite outside table, we have to have three or more people." She tossed me a wink. "So the story is that we lost our third person at the far turn."

"Gotcha," I said, smiling.

Soon I spotted the famous pink hotel. As we ascended the long palm-lined driveway, I got the tingles. I wasn't just visiting the legendary hotel — I was going there with a Hollywood legend.

"It's beautiful," I said. "Have you been coming here a long time?"

"Yes, *indeedy*. This is where we come to vote. We don't have to go to an old garage or someone's smelly back room."

"I can't imagine the people you must have seen here," I said.

"It was crazy. Everyone who lived in Beverly Hills came here, and *everyone* seemed to live in Beverly Hills."

We left the car with the valet and together made our way into the hotel. Somewhere a pianist was playing Gershwin. As we walked through the lobby, Ann noted that they'd recently done it over. "All the chairs are too big for just one person to sit on," Ann said. "The designer must have had a very big beam."

When we reached the lounge, I gave the name *Rutherford*.

"Table 725?" the hostess asked, checking the reservation. This was Ann's favorite table.

"Yes," Ann said. "Outside." Ann pretended to pout. "We're so sorry. It's only two of us today. We lost someone at the far turn."

The hostess gave me a knowing smile. She'd clearly heard this before. We followed her to our table and scooted into the booth. The table was dressed with a white cloth. Green letters on the pink sugar packets said *Beverly Hills Hotel.*

"Would you like to be evil and have a Bloody Mary?" Ann asked.

"I'd love one."

Ann ordered two Bloody Marys and an extra glass of ice.

"Why the ice?" I asked.

"Well," she said with a smile, "people assume that I want to weaken my drink." Her smile grew. "But really, I want it to last longer."

After a laugh, I looked around the brick patio. Mature palms and white umbrellas shaded the tables. Arbors spilled with bougainvillea, and planter boxes overflowed with hills of red, white, and pink impatiens.

"I expected it to be more crowded," I said. Besides us, there were only a few people in the garden area.

"It will fill up in a while. On Saturdays, there are more people here than a Polish wedding." The waitress set a plate of crisp-looking bread and dip on the table. "You'll like this," Ann said, picking up a piece. "It's noisy. I like loud food."

As I ate my noisy bread, Ann began rummaging through her purse like Mary Poppins. Then she pulled out a red pen and gave it a click. The end turned into a flashlight.

"Have you ever been in a dark restaurant and couldn't read the menu?" Ann asked. "Well, I have a Chinese manicurist who is very tough to get an appointment with. She had one of these pens, and I asked her where I could buy some. She said, 'I have no idea where it came from, but I can get some for you.' They are very good businesspeople." Ann handed me the pen.

"For *me?*"

"Yes." Then she pulled out a second pen and leaned over it. "What color is this?"

"Purple."

She gave that one to me, too. "Find someone who likes purple." After I thanked her, Ann said, "People love it when you bring them a little goodie."

As Ann closed her handbag, I noticed she was wearing a bracelet packed with silver charms, among them a silver book, a house, a thimble, and a pair of roller skates. Smiling, I reached out and touched the bracelet.

Ann stretched out her hand for me to see it better. "I've had this forever," she said. "Over the years, I've added charms to mark special occasions." Ann searched through the bracelet and found a silver lion. "I got this one when I signed my contract at MGM. My sister gave it to me." I scooted in closer as Ann searched for another. It was a carriage. She showed me how the door opened and closed. "I bought this for myself when I made *Pride and Prejudice.* I also got one for each of my sisters in the picture."

I touched a silver star on the bracelet. "What's this one for?"

"Bill gave me that when I got my star on the Hollywood Walk of Fame. I actually have two of them." She looked for the other one. "Here it is. One star is for motion pictures and the other is for television. MGM paid for one, and the other was paid for by NBC."

"You have to pay for them?"

"Oh, yes. Each costs about $15,000, I believe."

Ann told me that Mickey Rooney had three stars of his own and that her former costar Gene Autry was the only honoree to have five. "For the longest time," Ann said, "David Selznick never had his own star. He should have been one of the first to get one. Finally, a couple of years ago, someone got smart, and the oversight was corrected. They asked me to stand in for David. I was very pleased about that."

Ann reached into her purse, pulled out her wallet, and took out a plastic laminated card. A fan had made it for her. On it were the addresses of both her stars — one at 6333 Hollywood Boulevard and the other at 6834. "It's funny," Ann said. "Both my stars are just a short walk from the apartment where my mom, sister, and I first lived when we moved to Hollywood. As a kid, I used to watch the beams of the searchlights shoot up from in front of Grauman's or the Egyptian when the theaters held their big premieres. I'd try to imagine who was there and what they were wearing." Ann shook her head and shrugged. "Little did I know that one day, I'd have not one, but two stars on the Hollywood Walk of Fame." Then Ann held up her wrist and gave her charm bracelet a shake. "Look," she said, smiling. "My life on a wrist."

The waitress set our drinks on the table, and Ann ordered for both of us: tortilla soup for her and a sirloin burger for me. For dessert — two bowls of chocolate ice cream. Ann asked for an extra scoop in mine.

When the waitress stepped away, Ann reached for her glass. "I just love Bloody Marys. It gets your attention." She pulled the celery out of the glass and made a loud crunch. "And it's good for you, too."

After we clinked our glasses and sipped our good-for-you drinks, I asked Ann who her favorite actresses were.

"Oh, there were so many," she answered. "Let me see … Eve Arden … Angela Lansbury … Katharine Hepburn. I was not privileged to work with her, but I saw every picture she ever made. Anything she did just knocked me out. She almost sang her dialogue.

You know what I mean? I never knew what note she was going to hit next." Ann changed her voice to sound like Hepburn's. " 'The calla lilies are in bloom.' "

"And now you're supporting her costume collection at Kent State."

"That's right. I just loved Bette Davis's work, too. She was memorable. When you went away from a Davis film, you could still hear her. She stayed with you."

Ann took another bite of her celery. "I thought Bette was a wonderful mother to her kids. Her daughter wrote a bad book about her, but I wouldn't buy it. It's against my principles.

"Greer Garson was wonderful, too. Greer Dear, I called her. She was warm and lovely. Huggable. She hugged *you*, and she beat you to it. Greer Dear was the most special lady. When we made *Pride and Prejudice*, she had tea on the set at 4:00. In fact, it was she who taught me how to make a proper pot of tea: two bags, milk in first. One day, Greer Dear invited me over to her house for afternoon tea. It was all very lovely with a silver service, tarts, scones, and little cucumber sandwiches. She and her mother had tea every day. Her mother was lovely, too. You understood why Greer Garson was Greer Garson when you met her mother. There was such warmth there."

I didn't say it, but I felt the same about Ann.

Ann gazes at her beloved charm bracelet.
— photo courtesy of the Patrick Picking Collection

"Well," Ann continued, "right there at the tea I sat on Greer's glasses and destroyed them. Oh, I felt so badly about it, but Greer didn't give a rip." Ann took a sip of her drink and set it down. "Greer had a special dignity that she carried with her. It's no wonder she became the first lady of MGM. She moved so beautifully on the screen — not just her body, but her face, the way it caught the light. And that voice. She had the most beautiful voice on the screen. Yes, Greer Dear had that star quality that comes off the screen and arrests you.

"Today," Ann went on, "the word *star* doesn't mean what it used to. In the old days, that term meant the studios could count on your name selling tickets. Just the fact that you were in the film made it a good investment. That and only that was when your name appeared above the title. *That* was stardom. Greer Garson in ... Greta Garbo in ... Norma Shearer in ... People throw the word around so much nowadays that it has lost its meaning." Ann turned to me. "Who's your favorite actress?"

"Gosh, that's a hard one," I said. "I have so many. For sure Ingrid Bergman."

"Absolutely!" Ann cried. "I never worked with her, but I worshiped her from afar. And she had every hair on her eyebrows."

"Yes, she did," I chuckled.

"Of course," Ann went on, "I was enchanted with Vivien Leigh. We all were."

I tilted closer. "What was it like working with her?"

"Honey, she was the hardest-working actor I have ever met. I've never seen anyone work longer hours. When making *The Wind*, Vivien had to be at makeup by six in the morning, so she must have been up before five. She didn't just work till six. She'd work until seven, break for dinner, then come back and work till late. Vivien was the most vibrant, dynamic woman — absolutely delicious. She *was* Scarlett. When we were shooting, no matter what she'd just been doing — playing cards or laughing with friends — as soon as they called her to the set, she'd go straight into the scene without any moment of transition. Oh, she was just glorious."

"And Clark Gable — what was he like?"

"All man."

I cracked up.

"I didn't have any scenes with Clark." Ann grinned. "But I could look at him. Oh, God! Remember him in *It Happened One Night*?" Ann slapped her hands on the table. "I think I'm going to buy a copy of that and just run it." Ann's sigh was pitched high. "One could easily forget her lines when staring at Clark Gable."

The Wind

I was filled with admiration for Vivien Leigh. I had already seen her in two British films. The first day I met her was at a wardrobe fitting. That moment will forever stay in my mind. They were pinning her in the red velvet dress that she wears near the end of the picture. I couldn't take my eyes off her. She looked like a piece of Dresden china. And, of course, the camera adored her. It was impossible for them to take an unattractive shot of Vivien Leigh.

Most of Gone With the Wind *was filmed down the block from Metro at Selznick International Studios, formerly RKO. It was a good thing that David started filming at the beginning of the book because by the time Vivien worked two or three months, she'd lost weight. The apples of her cheeks had gotten flatter. When you watch the picture, you can see it. They had to take her costumes in because she was losing weight. She was in just about every scene, and back then we still worked a six-day week. Oftentimes, I saw her step out of her dress, whatever it was, and the wardrobe women would take a little in at the waist so that it would fit.*

After six months of shooting, when they were just about ready to wrap, David wanted to film the first scene again, the one where Scarlett runs down the lawn with the Tarleton twins behind her. Well, they couldn't shoot it because Vivien had aged so. There was no way she could play a teenager anymore. What many people don't realize is that Vivien wasn't healthy. She had contracted tuberculosis as a child and had never been entirely cured. Her lungs were weak. Neither George Cukor nor Victor Fleming knew it. David Selznick didn't know about it either. Vivien told me years later. She and I became good friends.

There were constant script changes during filming. Every morning they passed out new pages that had been written the night before. It was a very disorganized shoot. Each day, they used a different color paper so we could keep track. These were called rainbow sheets. When we got our new pages, some of the cast members would complain because they had already learned their lines, but not Vivien. I never heard her complain. She would look at the new pages and have her lines down in fifteen minutes. She knew them perfectly — and everyone else's, too.

Sometimes Clark Gable and I shared the same soundstage while waiting for our cues. I was enchanted with seeing him in the flesh. He wasn't full of himself, wasn't spoiled. He never strutted or swaggered. He didn't fancy himself a big star like some of the other leading men I knew. Back then, my acid test for an actor was — did the crew like him? And they did. Between scenes, Clark would straddle a bench, pull out a deck of cards, and play a hand with the guys — the men up on the plank, the boys on the ladders. He knew all their names. He was one of them. He had come up the hard way in a small coal-mining town in Ohio; he had nothing when he started. Being the star that he was, he could have closed himself in his dressing room with a pot of coffee, but he didn't. At that time most of the big stars had gofers, but not Clark. When they rang the bell for lunch, he stood in line just like everyone else. And he never let anyone call him Mr. Gable. There'd be none of that. He was Clark.

Hattie McDaniel was a warm hug. I think that's why people enjoy watching the movie. They're getting warm hugs in absentia. Hattie had a sister named Etta who was also an actor. We called her Ettie. The two looked just alike; they could have been twins. Before The Wind, *I had done* The Lonely Trail *with her at Republic, so when I worked with Hattie, it was like working with her sister. Gable had already done two pictures with her, too. I believe he put a good word in for her to play Mammy. Everyone knows about the intense competition for Scarlett, but there was also competition for the part of Mammy. Even Eleanor Roosevelt requested that her maid from the White House be tested. But Hattie got it. Later, she told me that some of her friends looked down on her for playing a maid, but Hattie said, "I'd rather play a maid than be a maid."*

Gone With the Wind *was the only picture I've ever been in where we couldn't wait to be introduced to the other actors in the cast. We'd all read the book. So, we all had pictures in our minds of what the characters should look like. When we met someone new in the cast like Belle Watling or Aunt Pittypat or Big Sam, we'd hurl ourselves at them and say, "You're just perfect for this role! If I had cast your part, I couldn't have done better!"*

The picture was perfectly cast. Thomas Mitchell as Scarlett's father lived the part. Barbara O'Neil, Scarlett's mother, thought out loud; she followed so closely. When I saw her lying in wake after Scarlett returns to Tara, I almost started crying; it upset me so. Little Mickey Kuhn, who played Beau Wilkes — Ashley and Melanie's seven-year-old son — was just right, too. When he arrived at the audition there were hundreds of boys, but as soon as the casting director set eyes on him she told everyone else to go home. On the set, Mickey called Gable Uncle Clark. He used to play with Mickey on the set. There's a scene in the picture where Rhett steps into the playroom where Beau is playing. They had to shoot that a couple of times. Mickey was supposed to say, "Hello, Uncle Rhett," but he kept saying, "Hello, Uncle Clark."

I worked on the picture for about five or six months, but never more than a few days at a time. Some days I'd shoot a scene for The Wind *in the morning at Selznick Studios, then work on another picture back at*

Metro in the afternoon. The first scene I filmed in The Wind *was the one where I run down the stairs with my sister Suellen asking my mother if I may go to the barbecue. It's the first time you see Scarlett's whole family together. After that, we shot the family prayer scene where we're all on our knees at Tara, and Scarlett is planning what to say to Ashley. I think I'm the only one in the room who is actually praying. Both of these scenes were directed by George Cukor before he was replaced by Victor Fleming.*

Clark was responsible for that. Gable was more comfortable with someone like Fleming, a guy's guy. Clark felt that all the attention was being put on Scarlett, and that Rhett was just a painting on a wall. When George was taken off the picture, everybody went into cardiac arrest. There was a great mourning at the bar. Too many of us had experienced working with directors in their funny little boots who didn't listen to the actors and just demanded that you do things. George was different. He was gentle. He listened. He let you rehearse. Then he'd quietly call you aside and discuss it. I was in awe of watching him work.

After George was let go, both Vivien and Olivia were devastated. But they kept right on working with him. When Vivien had a break on the set, she would go to the phone and call George. If Vivien or Olivia knew a big scene was coming up, they'd get in their cars and scurry straight to George's house in Beverly Hills after their day's work. We all knew it, but nobody told. George gave them a nursery dinner of a baked potato and a lamb chop or a piece of chicken, God love him. After the nourishing meal, they worked together on the next day's scenes. The following morning, Victor would say, "OK, ladies, let me see what you've got." And there it was. The funny thing was that early on neither Vivien nor Olivia knew the other was seeing George. They were each seeing him separately. When Olivia finally told Vivien what she'd been doing, Vivien cried, "I've been seeing him, too!" Cukor was directing them for free. Nobody paid him. He had gone through all their important scenes *together, but Fleming got full credit as director. They should have been double-credited. I never understood why David didn't insist on that. **

The scene I remember filming most vividly was the one in which Evelyn Keyes and I had to pick cotton. Victor Fleming directed us in that. A driver picked us up at three o'clock in the morning and took us out to Calabasas, about twenty-five miles outside of Los Angeles, where a field had been planted with cotton in different stages of growth. David had arranged with the owner to plant rotating crops. We got into our costumes that had been subjected to numerous beatings in the washing machine so that they'd look worn. David was obsessed with making sure the costumes looked worn and authentic. One morning, he showed up to check the sunrise. He was looking for the perfect one. Meanwhile, with our skirts safety pinned up and huge pockets all the way around, we practiced how the heck to pick cotton. Well, that stuff's mean. It has thorns! After David arrived, I marched over to him and showed him my palms. "Mr. Selznick," I said, "look at my hands!" They were all red and scratched. David looked down at them and beamed. "Ohhh, that's good. That's very good." He was so happy about it that I couldn't stay mad at him for long.

A great amount of time, energy, and expense went into making that cotton-picking scene, yet in the final picture it can't run for more than thirty seconds. That was David Selznick. He wanted perfection. Everything in the picture had to be absolutely perfect. Most producers riffle through a script and hand it off to the director, but not David. He knew every if, and, or but — wrote most of them himself — and woe betide anyone if they so much as added an article.

During filming, I never wanted to go home. When we weren't working on the picture, both Evelyn Keyes and I made any excuse to slip

---

* Selznick contemplated some measure of screen credit or acknowledgement for George Cukor and Sam Wood (who filled in while Fleming was out sick), but neither of them nor Fleming was keen on the idea.

on over and watch our cherished book come to life. We'd stand and watch the prop men wire dogwood onto the artificial trees at Tara or spread brick red dirt on the ground to look like Georgia clay. Rand Brooks, who played Scarlett's first husband, filled us in on what and when they were filming. Rand and I had already done a picture together. We actually went out on a couple of dates, nothing serious. Oh, imagine if Scarlett knew that her little sister was dating her first husband. Boy, would she be mad.

I watched the filming of the very first scene in the picture, where Scarlett sits on the porch saying, "War, war, war." It was an early morning shoot. I wanted to be there on the first day of filming. They ended up reshooting it several times after that. The day I saw it, Scarlett was wearing the green sprigged barbecue dress, not the white-ruffled one she ends up wearing in the film. I sat on the catwalk when they shot the scene when Scarlett throws a vase at Ashley, then Rhett gets up from behind the couch and says, "Has the war started?" I vividly remember watching the scene where Scarlett purposefully puts her new Paris hat on backward, then turns to Rhett and says, "How do I look?" I stood behind a tree while they filmed Scarlett surrounded by her beaux at the Twelve Oaks barbecue. Rand had a big part in that, and I wanted to see how he did. When he finally saw himself on film, he complained about how he looked. He said his chin looked weak — that it lacked importance. I told him, "Rand, that's why they cast you in the part." He hated his role so much that in the Academy Award race that year, he voted for Of Mice and Men. I watched George Cukor shoot the scene where Melanie is about to have her baby. George was sitting at the foot of Melanie's bed, out of the range of the camera. When it was time for her to moan, he'd twist her ankle. Years later, when Olivia had her daughter, she sent George a card saying, "This time I did it without your help."

The most amazing scene that I ever witnessed being filmed was the famous shot where Scarlett searches for Dr. Meade, and the camera, on a *crane, pans back to reveal the ground laden with thousands of soldiers. It took a whole day to shoot. Selznick did the impossible with that one. He wanted several thousand bodies, but couldn't get enough extras. He also couldn't afford to make thousands of soldiers' uniforms. But David was undaunted. He contacted those Civil War groups that do the reenactments, borrowed their costumes, stuffed thousands of dummies, and put the clothes on them. Then he had his crews attach strings to each dummy for the living extras to pull. In doing so, David was able to double the population. I'll never forget it.*

I remember shooting more scenes for the picture, but they were eventually cut. One took place at the dinner table. Another was a wagon ride to Twelve Oaks. A third was a scene where Suellen and I wait for Scarlett to finish getting ready for the barbecue. A total of twelve hours of film was shot before the picture was cut down to under four. There were several people whose entire roles were cut out. I doubt that any of the deleted scenes exist today, but wouldn't it be wonderful if someone discovered them? Oh, wouldn't that be something?

The Drive

Life is a great big canvas, and you should throw all the
paint you can on it.

— *Danny Kaye*

Ann looked at my empty plate and grinned. "I'm so sorry you hated your hamburger."

Soon the waitress cleared our plates and set down our ice cream. As we licked our spoons, I asked Ann what scenes in *Gone With the Wind* impacted her the most.

"There were two," she said. "One scene had no people in it — just a sundial. Do you recall it? On the dial are the words, 'Do not squander time. That is the stuff life is made of.' When I first saw the picture, those words made a big impression on me. I've lived by it ever since. I'm prompt. I'm on time. I don't fritter it away. The second was a scene where Scarlett and several others are standing in a room together. Scarlett is wearing her burgundy velvet gown. Everyone is tense. Melanie steps in and walks right up to Scarlett, but you don't know what she's going to do or say. Is she going to slap her? Olivia brought such grace into the room. The tension just melted. I was moved by that."

We finished our lunch with a story about David Selznick. In 1957, Ann got her American citizenship papers, and to celebrate, Bill took Ann on her first trip to Europe. Selznick would be in Italy at the same time filming *A Farewell to Arms*. "Will you be in Rome?" David asked Bill. "Oh, sure," Bill replied. "When you're there," David said, "I'll take you to the best restaurant." As promised, when Ann and Bill arrived in Rome, David took them out to dinner. During the meal, David asked what they thought of Venice. Bill said they couldn't see Venice on this trip. "What do you mean?" David said. "You've dragged Ann all the way to Europe and you're not taking her to the best place of all?" Bill said he couldn't do everything. Plus he had to get back to work. Then David looked at his watch and excused himself from the table. Ann and Bill waited and waited, but David never returned. Finally, the maître d' came over and asked them to meet David in front of the restaurant. They got up, walked outside, and there stood David beaming from ear to ear. Parked in front of the restaurant was a limousine with Ann and Bill's luggage stacked on top. Ann recognized the belt to one of her dresses hanging out of a suitcase. David had called the Excelsior Hotel and told them to pack up all of Ann and Bill's things as quickly as possible. David knew that every night at eleven o'clock a train left Rome for Venice, and he secured the caboose for Ann and Bill. Together, the three drove to the station, where David chortled with laughter as he loaded them onto the train. At five the next morning, Ann and Bill rolled into Venice.

"It was one of the most memorable trips of my life," Ann said, paying the bill. "There was no disappointment because there was no anticipation. I think that's the whole fun of life — being surprised constantly."

After Ann collected her things, I scooted out of the booth and gave her my arm. "You know," I said, "I will always remember this lunch."

"Well, I hope so," she said, pulling herself up. "That's why I made you eat extra ice cream. You gotta have ice cream."

As we stepped out of the lounge and into the hotel lobby, Ann stopped and admired some jewelry in a lighted glass case. She touched the pin on her lapel, then turned to me. "Did I ever tell you how I got my butterfly?"

"No. Was it a gift from your husband?"

"Nope. I bought it myself. I saw it and I wanted it." She petted the pin. "Her name is Madame Butterfly."

"You named it?"

"Of course."

One day when Ann was picking up a watch at her jeweler's, her eyes widened when she spotted the diamond butterfly pin on the jeweler's sweater. Ann stood transfixed. "Take. That. Off!" Ann said. The jeweler looked surprised, but she removed it and handed it to Ann. She had purchased several pieces from her before. Ann asked her if she could take the butterfly home for a "sleepover," and she agreed. "Smart woman," Ann said to me as we stepped away from the case. "She knew that if Madame Butterfly and I had a sleepover together, I wouldn't return it." That night, Ann sat up with a jeweler's loop in her eye, examining all the stones. She'd never seen such workmanship in her life. The pin was 26 carats.

The next day, Ann called her stockbroker and said, "You know that Berkshire Hathaway I was going to try and get another share of?" He said yes and asked if Ann had enough now. Ann said she had enough, but it wasn't going into his pile. She found something that would give her more pleasure. "It *happied* me," Ann said. "So, I bought it." Years before, Ann had purchased one share of Berkshire Hathaway stock for $28,000. Everyone advised her not to; they said it was foolish. After the stock skyrocketed, they all shut up, and since then they let Ann do what she wants with her money. "I think it's OK for people to run amok once in a while, don't you? I stopped buying jewelry after that." She paused. "I think."

Ann and I walked out the front door and waited for the valet to bring my car. When the car pulled up, Ann reached into her handbag, took out three bills, and asked me to hand them to the valet. After we got into the car, I commented that they were all two-dollar bills. Ann said that she always tipped with them. She gave me a wink. "Then they remember you."

When we pulled out of the garage, I asked Ann if she'd be willing to show me some of her neighborhood, and she agreed. As we drove around, Ann pointed out the former homes of several stars, including Jean Harlow, Loretta Young, William Holden, Cyd Charisse, Marlene Dietrich, and James Cagney. We drove by the house where David May lived before he and Ann were married. Dinah Shore used to live next door. David played a lot of tennis at Dinah's. Beverly Hills, Ann said, hadn't changed much since she first moved there. If a newer house stood on a lot, Ann described what the original home used to look like. When she didn't care for the design of a new building, she'd say, "Whoever put that hoo-ha in had more money than brains."

Since it was the end of October, several homes were decorated for Halloween. Ann said that many of the movie stars who used to live in the area passed out their own Halloween candy. Ann had already gone to See's and bought special treats for the kids next door. One October, when Aunt Olivia flew in from Paris, she brought her daughter Giselle. Olivia called Ann and asked if her stepdaughter Deborah would take Giselle out trick-or-treating. Giselle had never experienced it. So, Ann made Giselle a Raggedy Ann costume with the red wig. "She loved it," Ann said, "but I don't think she had a clue who Raggedy Ann was."

As we turned onto Roxbury Drive, Ann asked me to pull to the side of the road and pointed out where Jimmy Stewart used to live. Ann had played opposite him in *Of Human Hearts*. Stewart was one of my favorite actors. I rolled down the window, and Ann looked at the house with me. It wasn't Jimmy Stewart's original home. Someone had torn that one down and built another. Ann had been inside the Stewarts' home many times. Jimmy and his wife Gloria used to throw small parties for just two or three couples. One day, Jimmy told Gloria that he wanted a vegetable garden. So, she bought him the lot next door, and they turned it into what the neighbors called the Garden of Eden. "It was the nicest vegetable garden in Beverly Hills," Ann said. "And then some idiot bought it and tore out the Garden of Eden."

Years before, Stewart had dated Ann's sister Judith. They'd worked together in summer stock. The first time Ann met him was when he came to her house to pick up Judith. When Ann opened the door, she was disappointed. "He was so tall and skinny," Ann said. "I was expecting someone who looked more like Robert Taylor. After they left, I turned to my mom and said, 'He's not that hot.' " Ann swooned as I pulled back into the street. "But later when I worked with him! Jimmy was a brilliant actor. He always knew his dialogue, never bumped into any furniture. He had a way of saying his lines as though he had just thought of them."

"Was he your favorite actor to work with?" I asked.

"I had several favorites. Robert Stack and Robert Sterling were wonderful. And Errol Flynn was charming. We made *Adventures of Don Juan* together. Actually, Errol was the shock of my life. I'd been warned to watch out for him and to wear my track shoes. I thought I'd have to be on a dead run, but he was the perfect gentleman. He had a monkey with him constantly on the set. He absolutely adored that monkey. It wore waterproof pants and diapers." Ann began to snicker. "It was a very naughty monkey. Errol had taught it all sorts of naughty things.

"Of course Red Skelton was one of my favorite leading men, too," Ann continued. "We made three *Whistling* pictures together. We whistled in the dark, whistled in Dixie, whistled in Brooklyn — we whistled *everywhere*. Red came up the hard way. During the Depression, he used to participate in those horrible dance marathons where you got a few minutes' sleep every couple of hours. They didn't even give them time to go to the bathroom. People would come to bet on the couples, and Red would talk his way through the performances and make the audience laugh. Pretty soon, they didn't come to see the dancing. They came to see what Red Skelton was going to say. He had a gift with a spark. It was his comic talent that rescued him."

While making the *Whistling* pictures, Ann had to tune Red out to keep from laughing. "He just undid me!" Ann said. "He was so off-center that you never knew what Red was going to do next." The director, S. Sylvan Simon, would sit in his director's chair right under the camera with tears streaming down his cheeks, he was laughing so hard. To keep himself from ruining the take, he would ram a handkerchief in his mouth.

One morning, Ann awoke with a pain in her ribs. It was difficult to breathe. Ann's mother thought she was coming down with something, so she took Ann to the studio doctor. The doctor asked with whom she was working, and Ann said Red Skelton. "Go back to work," the doctor said. "Every time somebody works with that clown, they come in here with aching ribs from laughing so much."

Turning a corner, I asked Ann if there were any actors that she didn't like.

"Oh, sure," she answered. "Occasionally you find a lemon." Ann thought about whether she should name him or not. "Well, he's dead now, so I guess I can say — Wallace Beery. Now, I loved him on the screen, but to work with him? I can describe it in two words — im-*possible!*"

According to Ann, Beery would do anything to steal a scene. He'd scratch himself inappropriately, belch, or pick the earwax out of his ears. "He was known as a lens louse," Ann said. "That's what actors call people who are bucking to get noticed." Beery was also a kleptomaniac. He'd take things off the set before they were finished using them. They'd need to shoot a scene at a different angle only to discover that things from the set were missing.

Ann and Beery made *Wyoming* together on location in Jackson Hole, Wyoming. Ann recalled a scene where the child actor named Bobs Watson had to run in wailing. As tears streamed down the boy's face, Beery proceeded to take off his hat, dip it into a trough, and twirl it around in the water. "I couldn't believe it," Ann said. "He was trying to steal the scene from a six-year-old child!"

Beery brought his daughter with him during the shoot, but paid little attention to her. One day, Ann saw the girl crying and asked her what was wrong. "All my clothes are in the bathtub," she whimpered. When the social worker dropped by the set, Beery threw all his daughter's clean clothes into the bathtub and pretended to be washing them.

Ann's first scene with Beery was a full page of dialogue. He rehearsed it fine, but when they started shooting, Beery not only said his lines, he said Ann's lines, too. "He put it all together and gave himself a monologue," Ann said. She was so mad that she did something she had never done before. Ann shouted, "Cut!" Then she stepped into Mr. Beery and said, "Sir, I did not come all the way out here to be a listening wall for you. You did not rehearse that way. I came here to play a part, and I can't do it when you've already played it!"

Marjorie Main was also in *Wyoming*. "She was a real character," Ann said. "She brought along a big loud machine that would make juice out of any vegetable you squished into it." Main was a fanatic about dirt and dust, so whenever she needed to open a door, she'd pull gloves out of her bloomers and put them on. One morning, Ann and her mother drove out to see Old Faithful at Yellowstone. Marjorie went along. On the way, she took her shoes off because she liked to feel the rumble of the floorboards beneath her feet. She stuck her head out the window, inhaling and exhaling loudly. Within minutes, all her hairpins had flown away. At Yellowstone, when Marjorie saw Old Faithful start spouting, she dropped to her knees, shouted "Great God, Almighty! It's the coming of the Lord!" and began praying. Her father had been a revivalist preacher.

As we stopped at an intersection, I spotted one of those buses that takes tourists around to see the stars' homes.

"Do the tour buses come by your house?" I asked.

"They used to," Ann said. "When my daughter and stepdaughter were young, they used to hide in the bushes and wait for them. As the buses drove by, the girls would perform cartwheels and somersaults on the grass for the tourists. When Gloria was older, she used to take the tours with an out-of-town friend. As the bus drove by my house, the driver would announce, 'And this is the home of Gene Kelly.' Gloria would say, 'I don't think so. I've been living in that house my whole life.' "

Steve Lawrence and Eydie Gorme used to live right next door to Ann's. She said they had a terrible time with those buses. Eydie would no sooner go outside in her nightie to pick up the paper when one would come along and slow down. "They weren't supposed to," Ann said, "but they did. And pretty soon everyone would be hanging out the windows, and all hell would break loose."

In 1999, Ann was at a recording studio narrating a tribute to Mickey Rooney for Turner Classic Movies when she fell down some stairs and shattered her leg. She spent eight weeks in the hospital. "I went out for two hours," Ann said, "and was gone two months." When Ann returned home, Steve and Eydie had sold their house, and the new owners had already torn it down. After the surgeries, Ann had to build up one shoe and start using a cane. Still, she was able to find humor in all of it. "They always told me to break a leg," she said, "and I finally did."

On our drive, we stopped at the former Grauman's Chinese Theater and strolled through its famous forecourt of hand- and footprints. Walking around was like flipping through Ann's address book. She knew so many of the actors: Mickey Rooney, Olivia de Havilland, Charles Laughton, Danny Kaye, Marilyn Monroe, Rosalind Russell, Ava Gardner, Myrna Loy, Lana Turner, Esther Williams, James Stewart, Norma Shearer, Jean Harlow, and Gene Autry. As we stood over Donald O'Connor's square, Ann recalled seeing him perform in vaudeville when he was a child. "His brothers would clobber the life out of him with their hats," Ann said, "and little Donald had the audience in stitches. When you see him sing 'Make 'Em Laugh,' he was doing that when he was seven years old." When we stopped at Jean Harlow's square, Ann remembered the summer of '37 when Harlow died at the age of 26. "I'd only been at MGM a couple of months," Ann said. "The whole studio was in mourning." Stepping away from the theater, Ann joked that a handwriting analyst would have a field day with all those signatures.

Ann Rutherford and Jimmy Stewart in *Of Human Hearts* (1937)
— from the private collection of Miss Rutherford

Ann and Red Skelton from *Whistling in the Dark* (1941)
— photo courtesy of the James Bawden Collection

Ann Rutherford and Robert Sterling in *This Time For Keeps* (1942)
— photo courtesy of the James Bawden Collection

Ann Rutherford and Robert Stack in *Badlands of Dakota* (1941)
— photo courtesy of the James Bawden Collection

Ann Rutherford and John Shelton in *The Ghost Comes Home* (1940)
— photo courtesy of the private collection of Miss Rutherford

Back in the car, I asked Ann where MGM was. She said it wasn't far.

"Could we go there?" I said.

"You can't get inside."

"Yes, I know. We could just park in the front."

"I haven't been out there in over thirty years," Ann said. "You realize it's not Metro anymore. It's Sony now."

I could sense from her voice that Ann wasn't too keen on going. I'd never been on the MGM lot. It would be a thrill to go there with one of its former contract players. "We won't stay long. I promise." I put my hand on her arm and gave her my best smile. "It would happy me."

Ann saw how much I wanted to go. Then she pressed her lips together and said, "Well … for a few minutes."

It didn't take long to get there. Ann directed me around the streets of Beverly Hills and through Hillcrest Country Club. When we turned onto Washington Boulevard, Ann motioned toward a long high wall. "That's the studio," she said. I was excited to see it. As we drove along the wall, Ann pointed out the original colonnade entrance used by stars in the '20s. It wasn't used anymore. I was surprised when Ann said that the studio gave her the key to the original gate. When they decided to stop using that entrance, the studio seized the opportunity to get some publicity out of it and snapped photos of the guard handing over the key to Ann. She still had it.

Pretty soon, I pulled over to the side of the road with a view of the East Gate, the studio's primary entrance. From where we parked I could see the Thalberg Building, a four-story white building near the main gate. Ann remembered that it was being built when she first started at MGM. Back then, she said, they called it the Iron Lung because of its early air conditioning. Ann explained that the producers used to have their offices there. Mr. Mayer's office was on the third floor, and an executive dining room was on the floor above that. Ann pointed to the water tower in the distance and Stage 6 where the Metro-Goldwyn-Mayer sign used to stand on top of it. She said that some claimed Stage 6 was haunted. "No doubt," Ann said flatly, "Crawford's lurking around in there."

After we shared a laugh, I asked Ann what it was like inside the studio.

"The studio itself had no glamour," Ann answered. "It was just rows of soundstages and buildings. Many of the buildings were old. Some had been there since the days of silent pictures. It was a factory, but not the big horrible factory that you read about these days." Ann looked over at the entrance. "That factory turned out romance and heartbreak and beauty." She paused. "It was my passport to the world."

MGM, Ann explained, used to belong to Loew's. It owned theaters all over the country. "Then one day, the government thought it was a bad idea that a company like Loew's should make their own pictures to show in their own theaters." Ann shook her head. "I still don't see any difference in the Union Oil people drilling for oil and selling gasoline at their own Union Oil gas stations."

It was quiet for a moment. Then I looked beyond the gate at the studio. "Can you remember it?"

"Oh yes, honey. I never wanted it to end."

MGM

I 'd wake up at five every morning in order to be at the studio by six. My mother was always there with a tray. On it — toast, coffee, orange juice, and a three-minute egg. She'd hand me a thermos of black coffee on my way out the door. My first year at MGM, I took the bus to work. Marjorie Main also rode the bus, and we'd often sit together. She taught me to observe people, to watch their mannerisms, postures, and expressions. "That's what you have to do," Marjorie said, "or you'll never be a good actress." When Mr. Mayer found out that I was taking a bus to work, he was horrified and ordered me to buy a car. So, I went to the Buick dealership and bought myself a secondhand car for four hundred dollars.

Once I started driving to the studio, I went in a padded silk bathrobe. Many of the actors arrived in their robes. There was no point in dressing; you had to change when you got there anyway. On my way to Metro, I drove through all those Japanese farms on Sepulveda Boulevard. At that time, MGM was surrounded by strawberry fields and just a few homes. Those poor Japanese farmers all lost those fields during the war. My own gardener was taken away and forced into an internment camp in the Mojave.

When I got to the studio, the first thing I did was look up at the poster with my picture on it. Over the entrance stood a huge poster of Jimmy

Stewart and me in Of Human Hearts. *The original title was* Benefits Forgot. *They say it was Mr. Mayer's favorite picture. I think that's why the sign was up there such a long time. Fans would usually be waiting at the gate, sometimes young families from out East. They would thrust their little books with lilac pages through the car window, and I'd sign them. Oftentimes they'd ask me to sign as Carreen O'Hara or Polly Benedict.*

At the entrance, I was greeted by the guard named Mr. Hollywood. Believe it or not, that really was his last name. He was part of the studio's police force. MGM had its own force. They were trained to recognize all the actors and salute the stars. MGM's police force was larger than Culver City's.

In the early mornings, the studio was abuzz with people arriving to work. Metro had thousands of employees, including stables of producers, directors, musicians, writers, and designers, plus an army of carpenters, metalworkers, and technicians of every kind. In my time, the studio employed about a hundred actors. Half of them were officially designated stars. The rest were featured players. I was a featured player. Each morning, Crawford would arrive at the studio followed by a retinue of servants: a cook, a maid, a hairdresser, her secretary, and a makeup girl who would curl her false eyelashes. One day, the actor Melvyn Douglas gathered a couple of people together, and they paraded into the studio just like Joan and her minions. She was not amused.

MGM was a city unto itself. Behind the walls were a park, a fire department, a lake, a zoo, schoolhouses, a hospital, a barbershop, a chiropractor, a doctor, even a dentist. Everything one could need was right there. Other buildings housed the camera, sound, art, wardrobe, property, research, special effects, and music departments. Beyond all of these were the back lots with replicas of Paris, London, New York, and Carvel, the hometown of the Hardy family. There were railroad depots and town squares, jungles and formal gardens, mansions and castles, even the Great Wall of China.

MGM had over twenty soundstages on which they were always shooting or preparing to shoot. You could stick your nose into any one of them, or any rehearsal hall, and see it teeming with life. In the same week, Nelson Eddy and Jeanette MacDonald could be recording on Stage 1. Katharine Hepburn and Spencer Tracy might be rehearsing on Stage 3. On another, William Powell and Myrna Loy would be shooting a Thin Man movie. On the back lot, Johnny Weissmuller would be shooting a Tarzan picture, and Esther Williams would be splashing in a pool. All around the studio, actors strolled the streets in costume. There was an astonishment in the air. Limousines drove stars around the lot. If I saw a star like Harlow or Garbo sweeping out of her dressing room with her maids following behind, I'd gasp and hold my breath.

After entering the lot, I went to my dressing room and dropped off my things. My dressing room was located in a two-storied, barrack-like structure that backed up to Washington Boulevard. It had an open veranda running across the front. Myrna Loy referred to this building as the bordello, for obvious reasons. The younger actors had their dressing rooms upstairs. For a long time, mine was next to Rosalind Russell's. She was a kick, but her husband wasn't. Actually, he was a big pain in the tuckus. We called him the Lizard of Roz. Rosalind, Loretta Young, and Ann Blythe all used to go to the same Catholic church in Beverly Hills. Rosalind called it Our Lady of the Cadillacs.

Stars like Shearer, Garson, MacDonald, and Harlow had their own suites elsewhere on the lot. They came complete with kitchens, fireplaces, and living rooms. Jean Harlow's was completely white. The size and placement of your dressing room was always in relation to your box office. The biggest stars were on the ground floor. The second-tiered stars had to walk upstairs. Janet Gaynor used to have a dressing room on the top floor, but after she was nominated for the Academy Award for A Star Is Born, *they moved her downstairs.*

In those days, MGM was set up like an invading army. There was a first wave of stars, then a second to replace them in case they got difficult. Rosalind Russell was insurance if Myrna Loy caused problems. James Craig was in the second line of defense behind Clark Gable. Even amongst the stars there was a pecking order. William Powell once explained to me that Crawford was billed above him and Gable, but below Norma Shearer. Powell was billed above Robert Montgomery, but below Jean Harlow. When little Freddie Bartholomew had top billing in Captains Courageous *over Spencer Tracy, Spence was not happy about it.*

Next, I reported along with the other female actors to the hair and makeup department. It was like a large beauty parlor. The building smelled beautiful with Max Factor's scents floating in the air. First, someone shampooed your hair. We all had long hair then. After your hair was washed, they'd roll it all up, and you'd sit under a hair dryer where someone would give you a movie magazine or cue your lines. Then they'd brush out your hair, style it, and wrap it up in netting so that it wouldn't get messed up. All the women walked around with their hair wrapped this way. We looked like we had beehives on our heads.

Sydney Guilaroff was head of the hair stylists. He was a magician with hair. Guilaroff was the one who changed Lana Turner's hair to blonde and Lucille Ball's to red. I knew both women when they were still brunettes like me. Usually, one of Guilaroff's assistants would do your hair, then Guilaroff would come and check it. I remember when Lena Horne came to the studio, the hairdressers refused to touch her hair because she was black. So Sydney did it himself. He asked Lena if she knew someone who would see to her hair when he was unavailable. Lena recommended a friend who was also black. Guilaroff hired her, and she became the first black hairdresser in the union.

After your hair was done, you sat in an adjustable barber chair in your own private pink booth where a makeup man — I don't recall any women — did your face. The mirror was illuminated with lights. On the counter sat brushes, tubes of grease paint, and liquid body makeup. If your nose felt fat that morning, he made it thin. If you wanted a dimple on your cheek, he gave you one. All the contract players had mimeographed photos with detailed instructions on how to best make up our faces. There were tricks. If your mouth was crooked, they played with your lipstick. If they wanted to raise your face, they painted your eyebrows higher. To bring out your cheekbones, they used darker shades of foundation on the lower part of your cheeks. As you sat there, someone would bring you coffee or a Danish. You really felt like a queen for those thirty minutes in that chair.

I remember when they were shooting The Wizard of Oz *I watched them put Ray Bolger's Scarecrow makeup on every morning, Bert Lahr's, too. It took hours. And once I remember a lovely young girl sitting in the makeup chair getting ready for her first screen test. Her southern accent was so strong you couldn't get a knife through it. Different casting directors came into the room and looked at her intently. They plucked her eyebrows and plugged a cleft in her chin with something. Finally, someone with good sense decided that she looked more distinctive with that lovely dimple in her chin. That girl was Ava Gardner.*

By nine o'clock I was on the set. My dresser would meet me with my costumes for the day all ready and steamed. A makeup man with an extra set of eyelashes in his pocket and a hairdresser would also be there to freshen up your lipstick or stick in extra hairpins. The actors walked through a scene, whatever it was, in our robes. During this time, a cameraman looked at it with his little eye-finder and talked to his best boy and a couple of lighting men. Then we went away, and our stand-ins came on while the lighting men fussed with the lights. Our stand-ins wore duplicate-type costumes, not exactly the same, but close enough in color. Meanwhile, in portable dressing rooms set up on the soundstage, we had our hair recombed, got dressed, or sat and knitted a sweater.

The lighting was what took the time. MGM was famous for its distinct lighting style. The settings were bathed in brilliant, high-key lighting that gave the pictures their soft, glossy look. Key lights washed out wrinkles and double chins; you always made sure you knew where your key light was. I called it love lighting because it made you look so beautiful. The lighting men could make a Greer Garson, who was thirty, look twenty and girls in their twenties look like they were teenagers. If you were having portraits made in the portrait studio, two or three electricians lit you. These men were worth their weight in gold. You don't have glamour if you're not lit right. Sometimes they'd put women's sheer stockings over the lens to wash out your wrinkles. There was a magic to the whole thing.

We didn't begin shooting until ten or ten-thirty. Scenes were not filmed in sequence. Once they got a scene lit, they saved the lighting and shot everything that took place in that setting. For example, if there was a scene in the dining room, they shot all the dining room scenes together. Often, they filmed a closing scene within the first week of shooting. They also got rid of the expensive actors as fast as they could. If they hired someone from another studio, they shot his scenes first to get him off salary.

We shot until lunch. Since we only got one hour to eat, most of us went to the commissary. Eating there was like going to a good restaurant. The tables had white cloths. The food was very good. Mr. Mayer hired an excellent chef. You didn't have to go around and fill your tray. Waitresses took your order. You paid after your meal; there was no running tab. On the menus there were dishes like the "Clark Gable Special" and the "Broadway Melody Sandwich." Alcohol was not served. Usually you sat with your own group — writers with writers, directors with directors. The younger actors generally shared a good-sized table. I often ate with Mickey Rooney, Elizabeth Taylor, Peter Lawford, Lana Turner, and our stand-ins. In those days, there was almost a caste system in the commissary. The A players sat in one section. Mr. Mayer had his own private dining room, which we called the Lion's Den. When he walked through, you almost felt that you had to stand.

I remember the first time I walked into the commissary I tried to act nonchalant, but I was completely starstruck. The legends of the world were there, my heroes and heroines. I saw Lionel Barrymore tucked against the wall. Clark Gable had his table. So did Spencer Tracy. They may as well have been thrones — so many people who were so important. If you were any type of movie fan at all, it was like you were in heaven. I'll never forget when Jean Harlow waved at me.

After lunch, we continued shooting until the end of the day. We tried to finish by six, but if they wanted to finish with a particular set, you stayed on till later. Quite often we shot till seven or around then. Nighttime was busy at the studio. That's when they began constructing the sets and getting them ready for the next morning. They couldn't build during the day; it would have been too noisy. The crews worked all night to get these things done. If a prop couldn't be found in the studio's huge warehouse, it was made overnight. Many of the crew had worked at the studio since it started in the '20s. They regarded the silent era as the golden age, not ours.

I'd drive home in my padded robe and get home around seven-thirty. After dinner, I learned my lines for the next day. Each day you went to the studio with all your lines not just memorized but performance ready. There was no time to learn them at work. Learning lines was never a problem for me. I memorized them by simply reading the pages over and over. That's all I needed. I got to know where the lines were located on the page; I could see them in my mind. My mom helped me practice. She'd cue me by reading the tail end of someone else's line. She got such a kick out of it.

Studio portrait of Ann Rutherford — photo from the private collection of
Ann Rutherford courtesy of Marietta Gone With the Wind Museum

Ann walks with Adeline Reynolds on the way to the
MGM commissary (1940).
— photo courtesy of the James Bawden Collection

Ann Rutherford dines at the MGM commissary. Notice that Ann is having soup. Ann said that when female players were photographed eating in the commissary, they were depicted eating "delicate" food or seated beside untouched plates. Men could be photographed eating steaks.
— photo courtesy of the private collection of Miss Rutherford

Ann Rutherford is surprised on her birthday with a party on the set of
Keeping Company (1940). The crew presented her with a makeup kit.
Attached was a card reading, "Keeping Company with you is
alright with us."
— photo courtesy of the James Bawden Collection

Studio portrait of Ann Rutherford — photo from the private collection of
Ann Rutherford courtesy of Marietta Gone With the Wind Museum

A 1941 studio portrait of Ann Rutherford
— photo courtesy of the Patrick Picking Collection

Studio Portrait of Ann Rutherford
— photo from the private collection of Miss Rutherford courtesy of
Marietta Gone With the Wind Museum

Publicity

I'm letting no man handle my bank account.

— *Hattie McDaniel*

"I can still remember my first day at Metro," Ann said. "I was so excited. I sneaked into an empty soundstage and stood there alone in the huge, cool dark space. The soundstage smelled of newly cut wood and fresh paint, as they often did." Ann inhaled to absorb the memory. Then she turned to me with a smile. "I can still smell it."

Ann's favorite place on the lot was the wardrobe department. "To me," she said, "wardrobe was the center of the studio." Ann said she used to love standing on the cast-iron balcony that ringed the interior of the three-story building and look out at the racks brimming with costumes from every picture MGM ever made. Ann had a friend who worked in wardrobe, and she'd let Ann look through the drawers full of lace, ribbons, and trims, or search through the storage rooms packed with exquisite fabrics from Rome, Paris, and Switzerland — cut velvet, chiffon, hammered satin, crepe, and lamé. All the great fabric houses sent their lines to the studio. Sometimes Ann's friend would take her through the racks to see the treasures among the costumes, silk-lined pieces that Garbo wore in *Camille* and gowns embroidered with real silver thread for Norma Shearer in *Marie*

Antoinette. Satins and furs were often used for the top female stars because they felt good against a woman's skin — and the man's who held her. "If a woman couldn't afford a designer gown," Ann said, "she could always pay twenty-five cents and admire one in the movies."

As actors progressed up the studio ladder, they stopped going into the regular dressing rooms and had their fittings in Adrian's private salon. It was furnished with white, art deco sofas. On the walls hung his watercolor sketches. A maid helped you get in and out of your clothes and served tea.

As we sat there in the car, Ann looked beyond the entrance. "Oftentimes, if I wasn't working, I'd just wander around the back lots — through New York Street, the Spanish hacienda, and the French district with its thatched roofs and gabled windows. I went to the studio every day like kids go to Disneyland. It was like a fairyland."

Sadness had crept into Ann's voice. It was time to leave.

"Thank you for taking me here," I said, starting the car.

She gave me a thin smile and patted my knee. "You are welcome."

"You know what?" I said, changing the subject. "You led a charmed life."

"I did," Ann said. "Maybe that's why my friend wants me to write a book."

I froze. She mentioned her book.

"I know someone who keeps pressuring me to write one," Ann went on. "He's bulldozing me about it."

I didn't answer. *Who* is pressuring her? I wondered. What's his name? Whoever it was, she didn't sound happy about it. I suddenly became sad. Since Paul and I talked about the idea, I'd thought a lot about writing it, fantasized about it even. I'd imagined myself sitting with Ann in her sunroom or in the library at Selznick's favorite card table, typing away while she regaled me with her stories. Thank God I hadn't brought it up. That would have been awkward.

Ann's voice broke my thoughts.

"I acted on that charm," she said. "I encouraged it. I let it charm its way anyplace if I thought it might get me a raise, or a better part, or improve my life. At the studio, I always wore my lipstick and made sure my hair was combed. I was raised to put my best foot forward, to do what you can with what you have. No matter where I went, I did the best I could with what I came with. I remember after signing my contract, Mr. Mayer said to the new starlets, 'Please don't go out in public looking like an unmade bed. The people who see you in the store or the post office or at the cleaners are the ones who go to see your movies.' Back then, we never dreamed of going out in jeans and a T-shirt like the young actors do today. In my day, we called men and women who dressed like that kitchen sink actors — like they were dressed to wash dishes." Ann shook her head. "And when I was in pictures, people came to see what you *wore* — not what you took off."

Ann knew she was lucky. "Where else," she said, "could you go to work and have them pay such careful attention to you and give you nice raises and send you to the White House to meet President Roosevelt like I did?" Ann knew that working in pictures opened doors for her that otherwise never would have been, and she used these opportunities to her full advantage. At Metro, she had to work forty weeks a year. During that time, the actors had to report to the studio every day, whether they were working or not. The remaining twelve weeks was her time off. The studio could lend actors out and make money from them, but if they didn't, there were things the actors could do. "If you had any brains in your head," Ann said, "you'd do them." Ann turned to me. "Remember those magazine covers you saw? Well, everybody likes to be on a magazine cover, but it's not going to just happen. You have to *cause* it to happen."

The minute Ann finished a picture, she went back to the studio and saw Howard Strickling, head of publicity, and let him know she had time off. "Do you want me to do any holiday art?" Ann would ask. That's when studio starlets would jump over firecrackers for the Fourth of July or sit around Forest Lawn with a rabbit and colored eggs for Easter.

"All you had to do was use your imagination and give them some ideas," Ann said. The studio would send a limousine to Ann's house along with a photographer and a girl from the publicity department with a lap full of clothes. The limos had little roller blinds in the back so that Ann could change. "Then suddenly," Ann said, "you wind up on a magazine cover. And when you wind up on a magazine cover, a producer likes using you because he thinks people are going to come see you."

Ann would make other offers to the studio as well. She would get her agent to book her on a radio show in Grand Central Station. There used to be a radio station upstairs. When Ann knew that she was going to New York, she would ask Mr. Strickling's men if they wanted her to give any interviews while she was there, and they'd start naming the columnists in the city like Walter Winchell and Radie Harris. All Ann had to do was mention her last picture or the new one MGM was making. With any luck, she might get her photo in the Rotogravure, the color insert of the Sunday paper. That always made Howard Strickling very happy.

Back then, when traveling from Southern California to New York, one had to change trains in Chicago. Ann would arrive in Chicago in the morning then leave at six o'clock at night on the 20th

Century Limited for New York. Loew's, MGM's parent company, had huge offices in Chicago. The Loew's men would meet Ann and her mother then take them to lunch at the Pump Room. If Ann wanted to go shopping, they dropped them off at Neiman Marcus. At that time there was no Neiman Marcus in California. Then they'd pick them up and see that they got on the train for New York. "I must admit," Ann said. "I miss the days of traveling by train. It was like a vacation. Your friends would see you off in Pasadena with a box of candy or a basket of fruit, and you got on with a stack of books and put yourself to bed. It was very civilized."

In New York City, Ann would be met by at least four Loew's men. One would ask, "What shows would you like to see?" Another would say, "We have your favorite suite at the Hampshire House." Overlooking Central Park and within walking distance from Fifth Avenue, it was Ann's favorite place to stay. A third man would say that she had a car and a driver at her disposal. "They spoiled me rotten!" Ann said. If she were to attend any kind of event, MGM assigned a handsome man from its publicity department to be her escort. Ann said, "This man would have to leave his poor wife sitting at home in Brooklyn and take me to a premiere, smiling broadly as I was being photographed. I wondered how his wife explained that." *

On one of the New York trips, Ann's sister Judith went along. One of the Loew's men who greeted them was a man named David Simon. He and Judith ended up getting married. Judith bought him a typewriter, and David started writing. Simon became a successful

---

* Sometimes MGM's publicity department staged fake dates. The studio would drive one of their starlets and a handsome young man to a nightclub like the Mocambo or the Trocadero. There they would go into the restrooms and change into elegant clothes supplied by the studio. Once dressed, they'd pose for photos. After the photographer got his shots, the young man and woman would return to the bathrooms, change, hand over the clothes, and be driven home.

producer of such popular television shows as *Beverly Hillbillies*, *Petticoat Junction*, *Mr. Ed*, *Green Acres*, and the first two seasons of *I Love Lucy*. "It's too bad," Ann said with a smirk. "Nobody liked his shows but the public."

When Ann knew that she'd be traveling to New York, she would call up some of the New York theater managers that she knew and ask if they wanted her to visit their theaters. They were always delighted. In order to hit as many theaters as possible, Ann came up with the idea of rushing her around in an ambulance. With the siren blaring, it would race around the city, and Ann would hop out and run backstage. The theater would stop the movie, and Ann would get up on stage and answer questions for about ten minutes. Then she'd jump back into the ambulance and dash to the next theater. On a good night, Ann could hit four or five theaters.

"You see, Phil," Ann said, "it all came down to one thing: I wanted to buy a house for my mother. I was a child of the Depression, and we had very little money. My father was out of the picture. One day, he just walked out for some cigarettes and never came back. When I was a young girl in San Francisco, I remember my mother whisking me out of bed in the middle of the night because she couldn't pay the rent. That happened more than once. As a kid, I used to collect bottles to help support my family. I'm sure that's why I'm such a packrat today. I save everything. Bill used to roll his eyes about this. If he ever said anything, I'd recite my motto: 'You never know when you're going to need it, and it doesn't eat or drink.' "

When making *Waterfront Lady*, her first picture at Mascot, Ann worked with an actor named Jack LaRue. He had been a big star. Ann's girlfriends and she thought he was the next best thing to Rudolph Valentino. "Just his name sent you reeling," Ann said. But in this picture, LaRue had a small role. Ann went up to Joe Stanley, the director, and asked why Mr. LaRue was playing such a tiny part. Stanley said that Jack hadn't saved his money. He had a family and needed to work. "It taught me a lesson," Ann said. "That's when I bought a big purse and opened up a bank account."

There's a scene in *Pride and Prejudice* when Lydia returns home newly married and proclaims, "We're rich, Mama! We're rich!" Well, that's exactly how Ann felt when she started working at MGM. After her first six months at the studio, this child of the Depression was making $400 a week, then $500, $700, and finally $1,250. But even though Ann was making "pots of money," as she liked to say, she was still frugal. Her sole aim was to buy that house. That's why she rode the bus to the studio. Ann often brought her own lunch to work. She made most of her own hats and many of her clothes, too. Ann got to be quite handy with a sewing machine. Finally, she saved enough and bought a white house on Bentley Avenue in Los Angeles, a smaller version of the one on Greenway. "I paid cash for it," Ann said. "It cost $18,500, and in those days that was a lot of money."

The Raise

*M*etro was sneaky about giving actors their raises. Instead of going through your agent as they should have, they went straight to the talent. Mr. Mayer had Mt. Ida call you up to his office, where she made you wait for a good half hour so that you were a basket case by the time he was ready to see you. Finally, you'd walk into Mr. Mayer's office with your palms all sweaty, and he'd say something about the business not doing so well — even though it was — so the studio wasn't giving out any raises. One day, a young actress came into the makeup department beside herself with worry. Mr. Mayer had called her in and told her that the studio wasn't doing well and that they had to keep her at the same salary. She had just bought a new convertible. Another girl told Ann the same story. She'd just purchased an ermine coat. Neither would have bought those expensive items if they'd known they weren't going to get their raises.

The studio offered credit to its young contractees to buy cars and houses and nice clothes. Many of the actors took advantage of this, and each week a portion was deducted from their paychecks. The loans were handed out purposely. Those who took them had to go along with whatever the studio wanted because they were so much in debt to them. They had to take whatever part they got. Lana Turner owed Mr. Mayer buckets of money. So did Janet Leigh. They could never turn down a *part. Well, I wasn't going to be indebted like that, and I was determined to get my raises. So, I came up with a plan.*

Sure enough, one day I got the call from Mrs. Koverman that Mr. Mayer wanted to see me. I knew what it was for, so I grabbed my handbag and headed over to the Thalberg Building. Mrs. Koverman had me wait almost thirty minutes before waving me in.

When I entered Mr. Mayer's office, he was standing behind his desk. He asked me to have a seat. "Ann," he said in his fatherly sort of way, "we like you a lot and we have big plans for you. The exhibitors love you. We're going to pick up your option, don't you worry about that." Then he dropped his head and started shaking it. He was a very good actor. We used to say that the L.B. in his name stood for Lionel Barrymore. "But," he said, "I'm afraid we won't be able to give you a raise this year. We're not doing so well." Well, I knew that the studio was doing very well. I'd already made two Hardy pictures, and they'd taken off like lightning. My agent had told me how well those pictures were doing.

As Mr. Mayer took a seat, I opened my handbag and pulled out my bankbook. For weeks, I'd been bringing it to work for this very moment. "Mr. Mayer," I said, "but I've been saving my money to buy a house for my mother."

Well, I didn't know that I had said the magic word: mother. Mr. Mayer had a thing about mothers. He revered his own. The matzo ball soup in the commissary was named after Mrs. Mayer. Suddenly he got all misty eyed. He didn't even look at my bankbook. He stood up, walked over to me, and patted my hand. "Don't you worry your little head about it," he said. "I'll talk to New York and make sure you get your raise."

From then on, I always got my raises.

Ann Rutherford poses for "leg art" on the beach (1941).
During her time at MGM, Ann took countless shots like this one.
— photo courtesy of the James Bawden Collection

Ann posed for so many publicity shots on this rock that local residents dubbed it Rutherford Rock. Notice that she is wearing her charm bracelet.
— photo courtesy of the James Bawden Collection

Few MGM contract players escaped posing in their swimsuits.
— photo courtesy of the James Bawden Collection

Ann stands in her own backyard in Beverly Hills.
— photo courtesy of the James Bawden Collection

Poolside

I would rather lose a good earring than be caught
without makeup.

— *Lana Turner*

That evening as Paul made dinner, I told him what Ann had said about someone bulldozing her to write a book. "So, that proves it," I said. "You were wrong. Ann doesn't want to write one."

"Wait a second," Paul said. "Hold it. All that means is that she doesn't want this *other* guy to write it. She didn't say anything about not wanting a book. Have you ever considered that maybe she is feeling *you* out? Perhaps she's as nervous about bringing up the subject as you are. What if she asked you, and you didn't want to? Then *she'd* feel awkward. Are you going to see her again?"

"Yes. Tomorrow."

Paul gave me a look. "So this is your third get-together in one week?"

"Yes."

"Hmm," he said, chin raised.

I swatted him with a dishtowel. "OK," I said, "even if you are right, I'm certainly not going to bring it up."

"Fair enough," Paul said. "But if I were you, I'd start writing some of this down."

***

On Friday, my last day in Beverly Hills, I got to Ann's at ten in the morning. She was all ready to go and gave me a Greer Dear-like hug. She beat me to it. I noticed that Ann was wearing her charm bracelet.

"Did you hear me hollering?" Ann asked. I hadn't. "We have a second staircase in the back. On it I have one of those motorized granny chairs you can sit on to ride up and down the stairs. A television sponsor gave it to Bill. Well, that thing moves like a snail, and every time I ride it I yell, 'Faster! Faster!' "

Ann said that I wouldn't want to get near her coffee and suggested that we go out to the Beverly Hills Hilton and sit by the pool. It was just a few blocks away. Stepping outside, she spoke to her key as she dropped it into her handbag and called out to feed the cat.

On the way to the Hilton, Ann pointed to what she called her sidewalk. It ran along El Dorado Elementary School. Ann's daughter Gloria had gone to school there as a child. There used to be no sidewalk, so Gloria had to walk to school on a dirt path. Ann phoned the city and asked them to put a sidewalk in, but they kept giving her the runaround. Finally, she'd had enough, so she phoned them and said, "I wonder how many camera crews will show up when they hear that Ann Rutherford is parading with a big sign shouting that Beverly Hills isn't interested in keeping kids safe." Ann flashed me a grin. "I got my sidewalk."

At the Hilton, I parked my car in the garage and helped Ann out. I felt bad for not using the valet parking. I hadn't thought of it. It was a long way for Ann to walk, but she didn't mind. She said it was good exercise. Slowly we walked through the parking lot and into a corridor leading to the restaurant. A tune from *Funny Girl* piped through the speakers.

"Who's singing?" Ann asked, holding my arm.

"Barbra Streisand."

"Anyone who can sing like that should be put behind glass."

As we made our way down the hall, Ann and I passed large, black-and-white photographs of famous celebrities. The first was Grace Kelly.

"Did you know her?" I asked, stopping in front of the photo. Ann squinted to see who it was. "It's Grace Kelly."

"Oh, yes. When I lived in New York those two years, Grace and my daughter took tennis lessons at the same club. I used to see her all the time."

I shook my head. "Of course you did."

Next, we walked by a photo of Audrey Hepburn. "Did you know Audrey Hepburn, too?" I waited for another yes.

"Actually, I didn't. I knew of her, of course, but I never knew her."

I made a pretend announcement. "There's someone Ann Rutherford didn't know."

Ann stopped in front of the next portrait and asked who it was.

"I think it's Hedy Lamarr," I said.

Ann stood closer. "Yes, that's Hedy. Everyone wanted to be like her. Lots of women colored their hair like hers. She invented something during the war, you know. I believe it had to do with torpedoes. They finally awarded her for it. I heard she auctioned off all her belongings, sold everything down to her kids' socks."

At the end of the corridor, near the entrance to the restaurant, hung a gorgeous photograph of Lana Turner. Ann stopped in front of it and said, "Good morning, Lana," like she was greeting an old friend.

Ann and I entered the restaurant, and the hostess led us to a table beside the pool. We took our seats, and the waiter adjusted the umbrella so that the light wouldn't be in our eyes. After ordering our coffee, I asked Ann if she knew Lana Turner was going to be a big star.

"Oh, yes," Ann said. "All you had to do was look at that face and that figure, and you knew. Lana was faultlessly beautiful. You couldn't take your eyes off of her. She not only had the perfect face for the camera, she moved with such easy, natural grace. Did you see her in *Ziegfeld Girl* when she walked down those steps? No one walked better than Lana. The camera adored her. When they weren't gussying her all up, she looked like a ripe peach. Her natural coloring was so beautiful." Ann paused while the waiter poured our coffees. "The two of us had more fun. On our days off, if we weren't doing holiday art, we went shopping together. Lana always drove. No matter what sweater or skirt or blouse Lana bought, she'd get it in every color that it came in. She pushed money like a vacuum cleaner."

Ann began to titter. "Sometimes Lana and I were so mean. Do you know who Luise Rainer is? She won the Academy Award for *The Good Earth*. I just saw her recently. She must be over a hundred now. Luise could cry better than anyone in Hollywood. Lana and I made *Dramatic School* with her. Well, if Luise didn't like the way a scene was going, she'd faint. She just fell over like a dead dog. At first, everyone got excited, but it got to the point that when Luise dropped to the floor, we all just walked away and left her."

The following year, Ann and Lana made *Dancing Co-ed* with Artie Shaw. Ann thought he was dreamy, but Lana wasn't impressed. One day, months after they finished the picture, Ann was at home when the phone rang. It was Artie. He asked if Ann wanted to go out that evening. Ann covered the phone and whispered to her mother. "It's Artie Shaw. He wants to know if we can go out tonight." Ann's mother whispered back, "Absolutely not!" Shaw was much older than Ann. Plus, according to the Motion Picture Mothers Association, he had a reputation.

At one o' clock in the morning the telephone rang at Ann's. Ann grabbed the phone in her room, and her mother picked up in hers. Ann heard a woman's voice say, "Oh, Lucille. My God!" It was Lana's mother. They were friends. "That man hired a plane, and they're in Las Vegas, and she married him."

My eyebrows shot up as high as they could go. "You're telling me..." I softened my voice. "... You're telling me that the same night Artie Shaw asked you out on a date he called Lana Turner, then married her?"

"Y-*ep*," Ann said, flatly. "Tried her on for size."

"But I thought you said she wasn't that into him."

"She wasn't. She barely looked at him."

"Did you ever tell Lana?"

"No!"

The waiter came over and took our order. Ann asked for a Danish, and I had toast. When he stepped away, Ann said that Shaw had never put his hand on an instrument until he was in school. His family didn't have enough money to rent a clarinet, so he got one from his music teacher. Because of that, Ann supported the Young Musicians Foundation to help raise money to buy instruments for children.

Then I had a thought. "Wait a second," I said. "At MGM, if you weren't shooting your own pictures, did you watch other movies being made?"

"All the time."

"You were allowed to watch?"

"Well, they didn't exactly *invite* you, but there was a way to do it.

I'd sneak into any place where I could get in the door sideways. If the light outside the soundstage was off, you just slid in and hid behind a set. Then you tiptoed over to a piece of scenery until you were as close as you could get. That's how you did it — except with a Garbo picture. Nobody was *ever* allowed to see her. When Garbo was shooting a scene, they hung black curtains around the set so that no one could watch. Even the director and the cameraman had to look through holes cut out of the cloth. People used to try and sneak onto Garbo's sets, but she'd catch 'em."

Ann was making *These Glamour Girls* at the same time the studio was filming *The Wizard of Oz*. If she wasn't needed on the set, she would rush over to one of the *Oz* soundstages — there were several — and stand in the shadows to watch. "I couldn't stay away," she said. "We all went to see *Oz*. I wanted to play the Wicked Witch." Ann recalled watching them shoot the scene where Dorothy meets the Scarecrow in the cornfield. They used a real raven. The bird was supposed to sit on Ray Bolger's shoulder, but it wouldn't behave. It flew into the rafters, and they couldn't get it down. It gave them a heck of a time.

Ann Rutherford receives a dance lesson from Leon Errol between scenes of
Dancing Co-Ed with Lana Turner (1939).
— photo courtesy of the James Bawden Collection

Ann said she cut her teeth on the Oz books. "I'd read them so many times," she said, "that I could draw the map of Oz on the inside cover from memory." Ann claimed that the Oz books taught her how to read. Her grandmother used to read them to her. One day when she was reading one to Ann, her grandmother got up to answer the phone. By the time she came back Ann was already three pages ahead. Years later, Ann was walking down the street in her neighborhood when she stopped to admire a beautiful garden with an aviary. A woman stood out front. Ann told her how lovely the flowers were, and the two started chatting. It turned out that the woman was Maud Baum, the wife of L. Frank Baum, author of *The Wizard of Oz*. They lived in the neighborhood. *

"I'm *so* bad," Ann said, shaking her head at herself. "A few years ago, I attended the seventieth anniversary celebration of *Gone With the Wind* in Ohio. There were a couple of Munchkins there because it was also the seventieth anniversary of *The Wizard of Oz*. The hosts set up a small apartment for all of us where we could relax. One of the Munchkins came into the kitchen where we were sitting and started complaining. 'It took me eighteen hours to get here,' he whined. 'I live in a small town in Florida and I had to take a bus to a train that took me to the airport. Then I had to fly to Pittsburgh.' I looked at him and said, 'You poor dear. You should have flown by carrier pigeon.' " That evening at dinner, there weren't enough chairs for everyone, and one of the Munchkins didn't have a seat. So Ann said, "Come here, dear. You can sit on my lap."

When we finished laughing, I said, "Ann, you witnessed history. You saw some of the greatest movies in the world being made."

---

* Frank and Maud Baum's home and garden, known as *Ozcot*, was built in 1910 on the southwest corner of what is now Cherokee Avenue at Yucca (one block north of Hollywood Boulevard) at 1749 Cherokee.

"And didn't know it," she added.

"Did you keep a journal?"

"No. I wish I had."

"What was it like to go to the movies and see all your friends up on the screen?"

"I was just so proud of them."

At that moment, I noticed two elderly gentlemen looking over at us from across the patio. One of them stood up and stepped over to our table.

"Excuse me," he said.

Ann looked up. "Am I talking too loudly?"

"Oh, no," the man said. He introduced himself as Bob. "Aren't you Ann Rutherford?" It reminded me of the time I first spoke with her at the Roosevelt Hotel.

Ann smiled. "Yes."

Bob called back to the second man. "It's Ann Rutherford ... from *Gone With the Wind*." He got up to join us. Then Bob turned back to Ann. "It's an honor to meet you, Miss Rutherford. A real honor. You're one of my favorites."

Ann turned on her movie star charm. "You want to go steady?"

As the four of us chuckled, I wondered how many gentlemen she had said that to.

"*Gone With the Wind* was made in 1939, yes?" Bob asked.

"That's right," Ann answered.

"And the premiere was in Atlanta?"

"Yes," Ann said. "Actually there were a couple of premieres, one in New York and another in Hollywood. The Atlanta premiere was a three-day event."

"Were you there?" the second man asked.

"Oh, yes," Ann answered.

I turned to her. "Do you still remember it?"

"Like it was yesterday," Ann replied. "I remember the past. I don't remember phone numbers."

Bob reached into his shirt pocket and handed us both his business card. "We'd love to take you out to dinner sometime. We're Jack Nicholson's people."

Jack Nicholson's people!

Then he called the waiter over and said our tab was on them. The two men gave Ann gentle bows as though they had just spoken with royalty. In Hollywood — they had.

When they stepped away, my jaw was touching my Adam's apple. I sat there for a moment, dumbfounded, then looked over at Ann who was intent on buttering her sweet roll. Perhaps she's used to this, I thought. Maybe this is just a normal day in the life of a movie star. Or maybe she didn't hear them.

I shook myself out of the daze and leaned over. "Ann, Jack Nicholson's people just asked us out for dinner."

She smiled. "What a good idea I had to come here, huh?"

"*And* they just paid for our breakfast."

She kept right on buttering her Danish. "Oh, isn't that nice."

The Premiere

*I*t was the Christmas season of 1939. On the morning of December 13, my train pulled into Atlanta's Terminal Station. I was the first cast member to arrive. My mother came with me. We had just come from Lexington, Kentucky, where we stopped to visit my cousin. I stepped off the train wearing a fur coat and a hat that I'd made myself. Women always wore hats then. I loved making my own. Traveling with hats required special planning though. When packing, you had to work out how your hats would nest one in the other.

At the station, we were met by a group of city officials, photographers, and cameramen. The mayor of Atlanta, Mr. Hartsfield, presented my mother and me with large bouquets of red roses. Then, with a police escort, they drove us to the Georgian Terrace Hotel where most of the visiting cast would stay. Inside my room, a bouquet of flowers from Margaret Mitchell waited for me. She sent flowers to all the cast members.

That afternoon, they gave me a tour of the Atlanta Journal *Building.* I sat at the typewriter used by Margaret Mitchell when she'd worked there as a reporter. They also took me to City Hall, where I gave an impromptu speech to a couple of hundred employees. In order for everyone to see, they hoisted me up on a desk. I told the crowd about my role in the picture. I hadn't seen it yet. I explained that my part had been *minor to start with, so after all the editing I hoped I'd be seen long enough to at least go through a door. While I was there, they made me honorary Mayor for the Day, but that lasted for only a few minutes. As the new mayor, I gave all the employees in the room time off — with pay!*

Later that day, more cast members arrived at Candler Field. Among them were Vivien Leigh, escorted by Laurence Olivier, and Olivia de Havilland. David Selznick and his wife also flew in. Leslie Howard did not attend. World War II had started, and he'd returned to England. As the crowds cheered, Vivien and Olivia were also presented with large bouquets of roses from Mr. Hartsfield. On the airfield, the governor declared the day of the premiere a state holiday for everyone except the police force. When Vivien heard the band playing "Dixie," she did the cutest thing. She turned to David Selznick and said, "Oh David, listen! They're playing our song from the picture."

Soon the guests were whisked off to the Georgian Terrace. At the hotel, my mother and I shared a suite with Alicia Rhett and her mother. Vivien and Laurence didn't stay at the Georgian Terrace. Because they were both married to other people at the time, it would have seemed improper for them to stay at the hotel together. They stayed somewhere else. The Georgian Terrace was heavily guarded by dozens of men from the National Guard. I remember you had to have a special card to enter and exit.

The next day, I met a few surviving Civil War veterans at the Confederate Soldiers Home of Georgia. The building, near Grant Park, was a block-sized, wrap-around bungalow. The rooms all looked out onto a courtyard. The old veterans dressed up in suits and ties to meet me. All were in their nineties. As we chatted, one old boy presented me with a small corsage of roses. Not to be outdone, another excused himself and returned with some Confederate money. I still have that.

After visiting the home, I returned to the airport in David Selznick's car to meet the plane bringing in Clark Gable and Carole Lombard.

Emblazoned on the side of the aircraft were the words MGM's Gone
With the Wind. *When Gable stepped out of the plane, the fans went
wild. Thousands had gathered to see them.*

*Next came the grand parade down Peachtree Street. By then,
hundreds of thousands of people bundled up in coats and hats lined the
streets. The children of Atlanta had been let out of school early to see the
event. It was just starting to get dark; the streetlights were on. In the
motorcade, the officials rode first, then the visiting celebrities. I sat in an
open car with one of the coordinators of the event. Gable's car was last.
As we paraded along the route, bands played, and the screaming crowd
waved Confederate flags. People threw confetti from windows and
rooftops and telephone poles. Thousands of camera bulbs flashed in the
darkness. It was thrilling.*

*That night, the cast attended the Junior League ball at the Civic
Auditorium. There were a couple of thousand guests. Some original
costumes from the picture were on display. Several pieces were displayed
at various places in the city. On one end of the hall stood the facade of a
Southern mansion. Acres of red, white, and blue bunting hung
everywhere in the auditorium. Evelyn Keyes and I wore costumes from
the picture. I wore my favorite dress with the Grecian key pattern. As
they introduced the cast members, a spotlight shone on our boxed seats,
and we stood and waved. When they announced my name though, I
waved in the dark. The man running the spotlight couldn't find me.*

*The following day, after a full schedule of luncheons, press parties,
and receptions, it was time for the long-awaited premiere at the Loew's
Grand Theater. The front of the building had been covered with a
columned facade. Above it hung a huge oval medallion of Scarlett and
Rhett. Out front, a podium with microphones had been set up, and an
artificial lawn extended to the street. In true Hollywood style, searchlights
pierced the sky, and cameras rolled as the police did their best to hold
back the throngs.*

At the start of the festivities, a rousing ovation greeted a small group of veterans dressed in Confederate uniforms. One of them was the soldier who had given me the Confederate money. Wild cheers erupted as celebrities stepped out of the cars and approached the microphones. Clark Gable gave a speech, and Margaret Mitchell said a few words. Even I spoke briefly. I wore a pink taffeta dress that I had made myself. Over it, I had on my fur coat. I didn't borrow it from the studio; I'd bought it with my own money. The coat stopped a little below my knee, and I never thought it looked quite right. I should have gone back to the furrier and swapped it for something else.

The Loew's Grand seated more than two thousand. They scattered the cast. None of us sat on the side or down in the first row. Clark Gable and Carole Lombard sat near the front with Margaret Mitchell and her husband, John Marsh. They seated me with a young man who had won me in a contest. I can't recall his name; I remember he was tall. My mother sat a few rows behind me. I recognized the turban she had on. Everyone was decked out to the nines. All of the men were dressed in tuxedos and white ties. The women wore formal gowns and long gloves. The backs of the burgundy velvet seats were draped with furs, and the theater smelled like flowers from all the corsages.

The original program for the premiere had included faux oil paintings of some of the minor characters on the back cover — Suellen, Mr. O'Hara, and myself. Hattie's photo was in the lower right corner. But an assistant to the mayor of Atlanta told Howard Dietz, chief of advertising, that a Negro could not be in the program — even though Hattie was the third female lead! So, Dietz scrambled to reprint the program, and the back cover of the program we held that night was blank.

Because of segregation laws, neither Butterfly McQueen nor Hattie McDaniel attended the premiere. Neither would have been allowed to sit in the theater, stay at the Georgian Terrace, or eat at the same restaurants as the rest of the cast members. Margaret Mitchell's own housekeeper couldn't see the picture till it played in a theater for blacks. When I arrived in Atlanta, I was shocked when I got off at the train station and saw the "White Only" and "Colored Only" signs at the drinking fountains. I'd never seen them before. When I was a child in San Francisco and Los Angeles, we all played jacks and double-jumped rope together. In the Loew's Grand, there wasn't a black face in the whole audience that night — only on the screen.

Finally, an announcement was made that the performance was about to start. Those who were standing took their seats. The audience quieted as the lights began to dim. Then Max Steiner's magnificent overture filled the theater, and the heavy velvet drapes parted. When Margaret Mitchell's name appeared on the screen, the audience roared. The cheering swelled even louder when the giant letters spelling out Gone With the Wind *swept across the screen. People cried and hissed and applauded throughout the picture. I heard crying when the camera pulled back to reveal the thousands of Confederate soldiers wounded and dead at the train station. The audience clapped for the Southern music. There were cheers when Scarlett shot the Yankee soldier on the staircase at Tara.*

The picture ended shortly after midnight. After the lights came up, for a few beats, not a sound could be heard. And then, as one, the whole audience rose to their feet and started clapping and clapping. The deafening ovation shook the hall. Mayor Hartsfield got up on stage, and speeches were made. The cast members stood and took their bows. Lastly, Margaret Mitchell took the stage, and the house went bananas.

After the premiere, most of the cast members went to the Piedmont Driving Club across the street from Margaret Mitchell's home for a Southern breakfast with biscuits and gravy, chicken, sausage, and a delicious ham that they probably started cooking in 1937. It was the first time I'd eaten authentic Southern food. The party went well into the morning. Later that day, my mother and I departed for the premiere in New York. The other cast members had all left by then. So, not only was I the first from the cast to arrive in Atlanta. I was the last to leave.

Ann Rutherford arrives at Terminal Station in Atlanta for the premiere of *Gone With the Wind* on December 13, 1939.
— photo courtesy of the Herb Bridges Collection

Ann Rutherford leaves the train station in Atlanta. Notice the shadows on the ground of the people who had come to see her.
— photo courtesy of the Herb Bridges Collection

Ann stands on a desk at Mayor Hartsfield's office in Atlanta.
She is wearing her charm bracelet.
— photo courtesy of the James Bawden Collection

Ann receives instructions from Mayor Hartsfield on how to be Mayor for the Day. Notice Ann's hat that she made for the occasion. According to an article in *Radio Romances*, "Ann has always made her own cocktail hats, and she approaches her hobby briskly, armed with a hat block, yards of wire for frames, bolts of various cloth, and boxes of flowers, veiling, and artificial birds."
— photo courtesy of the James Bawden Collection

Ann Rutherford sits at a premiere luncheon
with Major Peter Pierre Smith and Thomas Stitch.
— photo courtesy of the Herb Bridges Collection

Ann dines in the Sert Room at the Waldorf Astoria in December of 1939 for the New York premiere of *Gone With the Wind*. She is seated with Thomas Conner Jr. Ann is wearing her locket.
— photo courtesy of the John Wiley Jr. Collection

Ann Rutherford stands with Tom Connors Jr. in the lobby of the Capitol
Theater for the New York premiere of *Gone With the Wind.*
— photo courtesy of the Herb Bridges Collection

Ann Rutherford dances with close friend Rand Brooks who played Charles
Hamilton in *Gone With the Wind* (1940).
— photo courtesy of the James Bawden Collection

Andy Hardy

Always be a first-rate version of yourself instead of a second-rate
version of someone else.

— Judy Garland

"Who knew?" Ann said. "Who *knew* I'd wind up in a picture
that everybody suddenly loved?"

"I've seen footage of the Atlanta premiere online," I said. "You
can watch the speech you gave."

"Do I keep yackin' and yackin'?"

"You seem pretty excited. Do you recall giving the speech?"

"I think I remember spilling my guts."

A few months after the premiere, Ann attended the Academy
Awards ceremony at Hollywood's Cocoanut Grove in the
Ambassador Hotel. Bob Hope was the MC. Judy Garland sang
"Over the Rainbow." Most of those in attendance knew ahead of
time who had won. Back then, the winners were made known to the
press in advance with the condition that they could not print the
names prior to the ceremony. Earlier that day, however, the *Los
Angeles Times* published the winners. *Gone With the Wind* swept the
awards. In 1939, no award was given for costume design, but Ann
was sure that Walter Plunkett would have won. Similarly, Monte
Westmore, makeup designer for *Gone With the Wind*, did not receive
an Academy Award nomination, as there was no makeup category at

that time. Ann recalled that the loudest ovation of the evening came when it was announced that Hattie McDaniel won for Best Supporting Actress. Hattie was not only the first black to be nominated for an Academy Award and the first to win one. She was also the first to sit at the Academy ceremony.

One day in 2006, a large box arrived on Ann's front porch. It was as tall as the door. Ann brought it inside and unwrapped it on her living room floor. It was a portrait of Hattie, the original painting used to make the thirty-nine cent stamp. The post office had sent it. Having no place for it, Ann wrapped it back up and sent it to Herb Bridges, the preeminent collector of *Gone With the Wind* memorabilia. He had written several books about the picture. "I was so happy when they made that stamp," Ann said. "Now all those people who had discriminated against Hattie would have to lick her backside."

Once when Ann was a guest at Scarlett on the Square in Marietta for a *Gone With the Wind* event, it was a madhouse as usual. The line went out the door as it always did. Ann was in the back signing autographs when one of the volunteers went up to Connie Sutherland, the director, and said there was someone in line whom she thought Connie should meet. The volunteer led Connie to a tall man standing with his wife. The man's name was Olen Gunnin. In his hand, he held a 1939 clipping with a photo from the *Atlanta Journal*. In the photograph, Olen carried a bass drum, and Ann stood beside him. Olen's high school band had been selected to play at the airfield when Clark Gable's plane arrived. While everyone was waiting for Gable's plane, Ann stepped over to Olen and signed the skin of his drum. A photographer from the *Atlanta Journal* snapped a picture of it. As soon as Connie saw the photo, she rushed over to Ann. When Ann laid eyes on the clipping, she remembered the whole thing. It all came back to her. Before he left, Olen said to Ann, "Last year, my doctor told me that I needed a pacemaker put in, so I did. But if I had met you first, I wouldn't have needed one."

When we finished our coffee beside the pool, Ann and I decided to go. Before we left, she slid a couple of two-dollar bills under her saucer. I helped her up, and we walked out of the restaurant, where Ann said good-bye to Lana.

Outside, Ann pointed to a big brass trolley that porters use to transport luggage.

"I've been known to put a chair on one of those and get pushed around," she said.

"Do you want one now?" I asked.

"No. I'd rather hold your hand."

On the drive home, Ann said she'd watched Atlanta grow from a small town to the Chicago of the South. Every five or ten years since the premiere, the city invited the cast back for a big celebration. When Ann was preparing to attend the fiftieth anniversary event in 1989, some of her friends advised her not to go. They said the picture had become jinxed. By then several of the film's key players were gone: Clark Gable, Vivien Leigh, Leslie Howard, Victor Fleming, David Selznick. But Ann wouldn't miss it. Over the years, Ann attended other *Gone With the Wind* events in Atlanta, including the fifteenth anniversary celebration in 1954, which she attended with Cammie King (Bonnie Blue Butler), and the 1967 rerelease of the film in widescreen.

Ann Rutherford rides in a parade for the fifteenth anniversary celebration
of *Gone With the Wind* in Atlanta (1954).
— photo courtesy of the Herb Bridges Collection

Ann Rutherford, Cammie King, and George Murphy with pilots at
Lockheed for the fifteenth anniversary of *Gone With the Wind* (1954) in
Marietta, Georgia.
— photo courtesy of Marietta Gone With the Wind Museum

Cammie King and Ann had become good friends. They often
attended the *Gone With the Wind* festivals together up until
Cammie's death in 2010. Though she was only five years old when
Gone With the Wind was made, Cammie had several clear memories
of the filming. She remembered wearing her blue riding habit and
the feel of the velvet. It was one of her first dresses. She'd never forget
turning a corner on the lot one day and seeing a short man dressed in
the exact same dress. And he was smoking a cigar! It was her double;

he rode Bonnie Blue's pony in the picture. Cammie also recalled Clark Gable's itchy mustache when he kissed her. Getting cuddled by Gable, Cammie said later in life, was one of life's ironies. Here she was kissed by the king of Hollywood — something other women would have died for — and she was too young to appreciate it.

Soon Ann and I were back at Greenway. Before getting out of the car, Ann asked if I'd like to come in for a glass of wine. Her doctor wanted her to have a glass of red wine at every meal. Ann said that she made her nephew, a wine connoisseur, crazy when she went to his home for dinner. "When they pour me some wine," she said, "I take a spoon and quietly drop an ice cube into my glass."

"You're not supposed to do that," I said, chuckling.

"Believe me," Ann said, "I've been assured of that."

I glanced at my watch. By now it was approaching four, and I really needed to hit the road. I'd planned to leave at noon. I had a seven-hour drive back to San Francisco ahead of me and still had to drop off my rental car and pack. My flight to Budapest would leave at five the next morning. But how could I say no? I didn't know when I'd see Ann again. "Sure," I said. "But I can't stay long."

"Good!" said Ann. Then, patting her pockets, she spoke of herself in the third person. "Did Ann say where she put her key?"

"Yes," I answered, smiling. "She put it in her handbag."

When we stepped inside, the Rubbermaid container was full from the day's fan mail. We walked to the bar where Ann showed me the wine and asked if I'd pour us each a glass. She suggested that we sit in the library, where she took a seat on the sofa. I followed her a few minutes later with two glasses of white wine, one with an ice cube.

As I took a seat beside her, I noticed a stack of black-and-white glossy stills on the coffee table and picked one up. It looked like she'd been in the middle of signing them. The photo was from one of the Hardy films. Ann was standing with Mickey Rooney. Around her neck hung her locket.

"This is how I first met you," I said with a teasing note in my voice. "On late night TV. By the way, it's because of you that I'm bad at math."

"Why?" Ann said.

"I'd stay up late on Sunday nights to watch an Andy Hardy movie then fall asleep during math the next morning."

Ann laughed. "We older actors owe a great debt to Mr. Turner on Turner Classics. Our grandchildren can see that grandpa used to be somebody and, in her day, grandma used to be a dish."

Smiling, I raised my glass to her. "To my movie star. Thanks for an unforgettable week." We clinked glasses and each took a sip. As I set down the photo, I asked Ann how many Hardy pictures she'd made.

"Twelve," she answered. Ann started listing the titles: *Life Begins for Andy Hardy, Andy Hardy Gets Spring Fever, The Courtship of Andy Hardy*. "They used every plot except *Andy Hardy Gets Bar Mitzvahed*." She paused for the laugh. "The part of Polly was perfect for me," she went on. "Polly's a parrot, and parrots like to talk."

But as much as Ann enjoyed playing Andy Hardy's girlfriend, she said it limited her. Directors saw her only as the girl next door. Ann would be up for a part, and a director would say, "Oh, but she's Polly. She can't do this." Ann said the studio didn't want to give her the role of Mary Thomas in *Keeping Company* because they thought it would tarnish her image as Polly Benedict, but Ann pushed for it and won. When Warner Bros. was casting *Mildred Pierce*, Ann so wanted the part of the daughter, but she didn't have a chance. "And to think," Ann said, grinning, "I could have slapped Joan Crawford."

The Hardy pictures were part of the B unit at Metro. MGM made the pictures in three weeks and shot them on what was known as New England Street out on Lot 2. The neighborhood had houses, a church, a malt shop, and a filling station. This was Carvel, Andy Hardy's hometown. Ann knew New England Street better than her own, right down to the doorknobs of Polly's house.

There were two producers on the series. Each month, they'd switch off giving parties for the junior players at MGM. It was always a formal dinner. "The boys had to get all gussied up," Ann said, "and the girls got fluffed up in their best party dresses." At these parties, the producers would pick the young actors' brains to find out what teenagers do.

Sometimes Ann would bring her boyfriend along to the parties. But one day she got angry with him, and they stopped going out. At the next party, Carey Wilson — he was one of the producers — said, "You don't look so happy, Ann. What's the matter? And where's that boyfriend of yours?" Ann said, "I didn't bring him. I don't like him anymore and I'm not ever going out with him again." Carey asked why, and Ann said, "Oh, he has a new Model A and all he does is pay attention to that dumb old car. And it's a secondhand one, too." Thanks to Ann, Carey got a whole Hardy picture out of that. In *Love Finds Andy Hardy*, Andy gets his first car, pays no attention to Polly, and she gets ticked off at him. *

The studio arranged other parties for their junior players. They liked to gather their young talent and photograph them for publicity purposes. Usually a photographer named Hymie Fink would go along, snapping photos of the whole evening. Ann enjoyed the

---

* Carey Wilson made up backgrounds for the characters in the Hardy series that he kept in a profile book. For Polly Benedict, he wrote, "address: 58 Newell Avenue, Carvel; telephone number: #3-881; birthdate: February 2, 1923." So, Ann was actually five years and three months older than Polly Benedict.

progressive parties the most. The guests would gather at Ann's, then head off to the Brown Derby for shrimp cocktail. Next, they'd all hop into a bus and drive to another restaurant for salad. Then they'd go to an Italian place downtown for spaghetti. Finally, they'd all end up at Ocean Park pier where they'd be given oversized pajamas and ride the slides until three o'clock in the morning.

The Hardy series was dynamite at the box office. It made millions for the studio. Mr. Mayer once told Ann that *Judge Hardy and Son* made more money than Garbo's *Ninotchka*. In 1943, the series won a special Oscar for its all-American wholesomeness. Mayer never allowed the production staff to tamper with the series' simplicity and homey virtues. Ann said that someone at the studio suggested that they combine the Hardy series with *Dr. Kildare*, another popular Metro series, by having Mickey Rooney seek the doctor's help after contracting a social disease. When L. B. heard this, he nearly had a seizure.

The Hardy pictures were often a showcase for the studio's new talent. Ann worked with several of Metro's contract players before they became stars, including Lana Turner, Esther Williams, Judy Garland, Kathryn Grayson, and Donna Reed. About the Hardy pictures, Mickey Rooney once said, "This was in fact a standard studio recipe. Take one young actress, pluck her eyebrows, cap her teeth, shape her hairline, pad as required, and throw them in the ring with Andy Hardy. Then wait and see."

According to Ann, the series' success was completely due to Mickey Rooney. "Mickey had more talent than the law allows," she said. Ann felt Mickey should have been a director. On Saturdays, the studio allowed him to direct tests. They didn't want to bring in some expensive director just to run a test, so they'd let Mickey do it. Ann said he was wonderful at it. Often when shooting the Hardy pictures,

Mickey would finish rehearsing a scene, then go up to George Seitz, the director, twist his sleeve, and say, "Uncle George, I've got an idea. What if we ...?" And then Mickey would come up with some funny business that they'd use in the picture. Ann said, "Those were the scenes that got the laughs."

After the first three Hardy pictures, MGM's big brass realized that they had a blockbuster on their hands, so Mayer decided to give the series the "A treatment." He extended the schedule from three weeks to three months. He also removed George Seitz and called in Woody Van Dyke. He'd directed a couple of Gable pictures. But Van Dyke wouldn't listen to Mickey's ideas. When Mickey tried suggesting something, Van Dyke would say, "Go away, kid. You're bothering me." There was no way Mickey was going to call him Uncle Woody. After a couple of weeks, the studio heads saw that they'd made a big mistake. They had absolutely nothing. The spark was gone. So, they scrapped it all, called back Seitz, and went back to the old schedule. "What they'd failed to understand," Ann said, "was that Mickey was the key to those first three pictures."

Rooney, Ann explained, was actually not the original Andy Hardy. The role was supposed to go to a young man named Frankie Thomas, but Thomas had a growth spurt and towered over Ann, who had already been cast. The producers thought it would be funnier if Andy's girlfriend were a little taller than him, so they gave the part to Mickey. Over time, Ann continued to grow, so during filming she'd have to slouch or remove her shoes. She did a lot of scenes in her stocking feet. If Ann and Mickey were walking down the street together, Ann walked in a trench. *

---

* Though Ann was not in *A Family Affair*, the first Hardy picture, she was supposed to be in it. Ann was working on *The Devil is Driving* at Columbia when Richard Dix tripped and broke his arm. This delayed the shoot, causing Ann to be

Ann said Mickey was also musically gifted. If they had an orchestra on the Hardy set for the school band, Mickey would wander around from chair to chair during the break and get music out of every instrument. Once Ann was in her dressing room when she heard this incredible tenor voice. Her father had been a tenor. Ann rushed out to see who it was. Mickey's dressing room door was open, and Ann asked him who'd been singing. Mickey said, "I was." He was trying to see if he could sound like Caruso.

One day when Mickey, Ann, and some friends were sitting in the commissary, Mickey got up in the middle of lunch to leave. Later, Ann gave him a hard time about it. "Oh, you think you're too special to eat with us," she said. Mickey felt bad, so he took Ann to the abandoned one-room schoolhouse (not the red schoolhouse where the junior players went to school) to show why he'd left. Inside the building, the desks were gone. A beat-up piano stood against the wall. Mickey introduced Ann to a man with a heavy accent named Eugene and said that he was his musical stenographer. "Why do you need a stenographer?" Ann asked, surprised. Mickey explained that he was working on a composition. He would play what he wanted on the piano. Then Eugene would lean over, correct a chord, and write down the music. Mickey didn't know one note of music from another. He played by ear.

When Mickey made *Young Tom Edison* in 1940, he went out to Edison, New Jersey, for the premiere. Mr. Ford, founder of the Ford Motor Company, held a dinner party for the cast. During the party, Mickey stepped over to the piano and started playing. Mr. Ford asked Mickey the name of the piece, and Mickey said, "I haven't named it yet."

---

unavailable. Margaret Marquis replaced her for the one picture. Ann's first appearance in a Hardy picture was *You're Only Young Once* in 1937.

"What do you mean *you* haven't named it?" said Mr. Ford.

"Well," Mickey replied, "I haven't."

"Did *you* compose this?"

Mickey shrugged. "Uh … yeah. I guess so. I don't write music, but I play this."

"Has it occurred to you," said Mr. Ford, "that we have *The Ford Sunday Evening Hour* on the radio?"

"Yeah. I've heard of it."

"Well, if you'd like to do a little more work on it and can stretch it to an hour, we would be honored to play it."

Mickey eventually performed it on the radio, but the studio didn't give him any publicity for it, which Ann thought was a major error. "Sometimes," she said, "they were behind the door when the brains were passed out."

Outwardly, Ann said, Mickey was self-assured, extremely confident, but she saw another side of him. Once on the set, Mickey was all excited to go to a football game after lunch, but an actor had to be replaced, and the schedule changed. Mickey would have to miss the game. When the director told Mickey that he'd have to stay, Mickey started crying. "Here he was the number-one box office star in the world," Ann said, "and suddenly he's a boy devastated because he can't go to a ball game."

Years after Ann retired from pictures, Mickey called Ann and asked if she'd play Polly in *Andy Hardy Comes Home*. Ann declined. "Everything has a season," she said to him. "It had its place in the sun." The script said that Polly and Andy were married and that Andy had become a judge. Ann told Mickey that few people marry their childhood sweethearts, so that counted her out. Plus, she didn't believe Andy would come back as Judge Hardy. He would have grown up to be a Bob Hope or a Red Skelton.

Ann took a sip of her wine. "Some people say that the Hardy pictures depicted an unreal world," she said, "but to me it wasn't unreal. The boys I dated in high school dressed like Andy Hardy. Maybe they didn't wear ties and pocket squares, but they took pride in their appearance. They didn't have any money — no one did in those days — but their shirts were starched and their hair was wet-combed. My girlfriends and I wore bows in our hair and dabbed perfume behind our ears just like Polly did." Ann smiled. "The only difference was that on screen I got to wear red nail polish. In real life, my girlfriends and I wore neutral-colored polish. Our mothers would have gotten after us if we wore red."

Ann continued. "Do you know who Lewis Stone is?" Stone played Andy Hardy's father. He had once been a star in silent pictures. "One day, Mr. Stone took me aside on the set and said, 'Ann, I see how much fun you're having here, and I want to give you some advice. Be a featured player as long as you can.' A featured player is not the star. Their names are never over the title. 'Don't aspire to be a star,' he advised. 'Stars peter out. A star's shoulders are saddled with the weight of the picture. If you remain a featured player, you can last in this business as long as you stand up, as long as you want to do it.' " Ann swirled the ice cube in her glass. "It all made sense to me. I took his advice to heart."

"You didn't want to be a star?" I asked, surprised.

"No. I'd seen what was happening to Mickey and Judy. Those two were worked like dogs. After shooting all day, they were expected to make publicity appearances and give interviews. Judy also did a lot of radio shows in the evenings. Sometimes she had to work till eleven or twelve at night. That meant she was expected to be as fresh in the last take as she'd been in the morning. Then she and Mickey had to get home, grab dinner, and memorize their lines for the next day's shoot. The minute they finished a picture they were on the train to the Midwest and the East, where they performed several shows a day. Once they hit New York, they had to do seven shows a day at the Capitol. Seven shows! Can you imagine? Simultaneously they were learning material for their next picture.

"I had my mother to protect me, but not Judy. Her mother was an idiot. I wouldn't be surprised if the studio wasn't paying her under the table to let Judy stay late and work. Judy was supporting her *and* her two sisters — the whole lot of them. On top of all this, the studio was constantly riding her about her weight. During *Oz*, Margaret Hamilton used to sneak cookies into Judy's dressing room. They had her on a starvation diet."

"Did they make you diet?"

"No. Never. I had good genes. My mother was slim. It never occurred to me to eat a whole hamburger, and I steered away from mashed potatoes and gravy. But at the studio you were constantly being watched. The eyes were always on you. There was pressure on all the actresses to stay slim — from the good old boys who watched the daily rushes. Oh, they tried to be tactful about it, but if they saw that you were 'pudging' out, they sent someone down to tell you to drop a size or two. They were very serious about it. They knew what the public wanted."

Ann saw this happen to Cecilia Parker, who played Andy Hardy's older sister. Cecilia had gained some weight, and a man came down to the Hardy set and told her to lose it. She cried to Ann about it. Soon after that, Parker left pictures.

The first time Ann met Garland at the studio was in MGM's wardrobe department. Judy hadn't done much at the studio yet. She was standing in the center of the room, tears running down her cheeks. Two fitters had laced her into a tight corset, the kind of heavy canvas piece used by portly women, and were tugging, trying to get a waist out of her. "It's too tight," Judy cried. "It's too tight." Ann couldn't bear watching it. Finally, she turned to the women and said, "For God's sake. Leave the poor kid alone!"

Judy Garland

*I*t was an afternoon I will never forget. My sister and I were sitting
and eating candy in the Pantages Theater in Los Angeles at the first
matinee. We were watching the vaudeville before the picture. This was
back in the days when every picture had a vaudeville show before it. After
the first act, the card announcing the next number flipped on the side of
the stage. It said "The Gumm Sisters." The piano started playing, and
out pranced three girls dressed in frilly costumes, the youngest, with her
little Dutch bob, pulling up the rear. Her name was Frances. She was
probably no more than eight or nine years old. She was the bubble gum.

After all three tap-danced, the littlest girl stepped forward and began
singing "I'll Get By." Immediately my sister and I looked at each other,
and I grabbed her arm. The girl's voice was so rich and powerful. There
was something electric about it. It touched you like a charged wire. You
couldn't believe it. When you experience something like that, it's a thrill
beyond everything you can imagine. When she finished singing, the
audience roared.

The next time I saw her was at a party at MGM. She was already
under contract. Her name was Judy Garland by then. The studio had
transformed the largest soundstage, Stage 25, into a giant nightclub for
hundreds of distributors and exhibitors. Once a year, the studio brought
them out for a week of previews and parties. We called them hat wearers;

they all wore hats. Many of the studio's contract players were at the party. Part of our job was to attend such events and mingle with the guests. Even some of the big stars like Gable were there.

When it was time for the entertainment, Judy got up from her chair and walked to a low stage. She wore a white organdy dress with ruffled shoulders. A piano stood on the side. No one really knew her; she hadn't done much up till then. On the platform sat a chair, a desk, and her little props — a pencil, a piece of paper, and a framed photo of Clark Gable. A single spot shone on her, and the pianist played the introduction. And then she started singing, "Dear Mr. Gable, I am writing this to you ..."

I'm telling you the whole place was in tears. Judy's heart was in her voice. As soon as she finished, the audience went crazy. Gable walked up to her and gave her a hug. She'd performed the song a few weeks earlier for his birthday. The hat wearers converged on Mr. Mayer. "Do something with that kid!" they cried. As the men surrounded Mr. Mayer, I spotted two of them walk up to the desk where Judy had been sitting. One swiped the paper she'd written on. Another took the pencil. They knew she was going to be a star. We all did.

Ann Rutherford with Mickey Rooney, Judy Garland and Lana Turner in
Love Finds Andy Hardy (1938). Ann is wearing her charm bracelet.
— photo courtesy of the private collection of Miss Rutherford

Mickey Rooney, Ann Rutherford, Judy Garland, Jackie Cooper, and Marjorie Gestring, U.S. Women's High Diving Champion of 1939, at Louis B. Mayer's beach house in Santa Monica for Garland's seventeenth birthday party.
— photo courtesy of the private collection of Miss Rutherford

Publicity still of Ann Rutherford and Mickey Rooney in *Andy Hardy Meets Debutante* (1940). Ann is wearing her charm bracelet.
— photo courtesy of the Patrick Picking Collection

The Coat

Look at this street, all cardboard, all phony, all done with mirrors. I like it better than any street in the world.

— *Sunset Boulevard*

"I was happy when Judy married David Rose and got away from her mother," Ann said. "They lived down the road. I don't know whatever happened to her sisters. They must have made them into lamps or something." Ann gave a little chuckle. "I remember during the war when we had air raid drills, we had a British warden in our neighborhood who'd go from house to house, making sure not a smidge of light could be seen. He took his job very seriously. God help you if any light escaped from your windows. Well, when the blackout sirens rang, Judy and I would call each other and warn one another that the warden was coming. She couldn't see my house, but she'd still say, 'Ann, I see light coming from your windows. You're going to get into trouble.' We got such a kick out of doing that."

Then Ann told me a story about Judy. "Once, back in the '60s, a friend of mine was driving with Judy through West Hollywood. Judy had a drink in her hand …"

"In the *car*?" I interrupted.

"Yes. She wanted a pack of cigarettes. There was a gay bar nearby. I believe it was the only one at the time. My friend knew there was a cigarette machine there, so he drove to the bar. Judy and he got out and walked inside. She bought her cigarettes, and the two walked out. When she got back into the car, Judy said, 'Damn, I forgot my drink.' My friend ran in to get it for her. He remembered that she'd set it on the top of the cigarette machine. Inside, a group of men swarmed him and asked if that had been Judy Garland. He said yes. Then he looked for her drink on top of the cigarette machine, but it wasn't there. He walked over to the bartender and asked if he knew what happened to it. The bartender motioned to the end of the counter. There, resting on a makeshift pedestal under a single spotlight, sat Judy's drink."

I burst out laughing.

"Oh, I almost forgot," Ann said, slapping her knees. "I have some things for you. They're over there on the table. Would you mind getting them?"

I stepped over to the table and smiled. "My egg cartons!" There were three of them.

"There's a book for you, too," Ann said.

I picked it up. The title was *MGM: Hollywood's Greatest Backlot*.

"Thank you," I said, returning with my gifts.

"You're so welcome. When the book first came out, I bought a bunch of copies and gave them to everyone I loved who had a coffee table. The book shows many of the buildings in the studio and all the back lots." Ann shook her head and sighed. "It's all gone now. They sold it off for real estate, then bulldozed every last inch of it. When I think of the history that was wiped away, it breaks my heart. The men running the studio weren't interested in preservation, just money. I hear that the only remnants on the lot that bear the MGM name are a couple of manhole covers. It's such a terrible shame. All they had to do was drive people around in a little tram like they do at

Universal and show them Andy Hardy's house, Esther Williams' pool, and Tarzan's jungle. It was all there — Katharine Hepburn's house in *The Philadelphia Story*, the train station where Garbo coughed her life out in *Camille*. At the end of the tour, they could have turned on the sprinklers where Gene Kelly sang 'Singin' in the Rain' and let some tap dancer hang on the lamppost. The tourists would have come."

"*I* would have," I said. "Actually, I would have been the guy on the lamppost."

"See," Ann said. "Oh, I realize that things have to change, but some things just shouldn't." She pointed to Debbie Reynolds' name on the cover of the book. She had written the foreword. "That dear little thing. Debbie was so undone when MGM held their auctions. In 1970, the studio sold off all their property. For ten days, they unloaded cars and costumes and furniture — everything. I watched the gavel fall on the Wicked Witch's hat, Andy Hardy's jalopy, even the *Cotton Blossom* from *Show Boat*. Oh, it was so sad. During the auction, I remember hearing that gorgeous score from *An American in Paris* over the PA system while at the same time all the picture's glorious costumes were being auctioned away.

"Debbie tried desperately to save as many of the costumes as she could," Ann continued. "She spent hundreds of thousands on pieces from important films. Later, she tried to raise money for a museum, but nobody in this miserable town would help her. Not long ago, she finally auctioned off the whole collection. She even had one of my dresses from *Pride and Prejudice*. I went to support her." Ann looked up at me, pushing a smile on her face. "I'm sorry," she said. "I didn't mean to sound so depressing."

"It depresses me, too," I said. "God, I wish I lived back then."

"You're not alone. Not a day goes by when I don't receive letters from people just like you. They're hungry for pictures with beauty and uplift and characters they can care about. Many are young people who have just discovered the older films. They say they don't like the pictures of today."

Ann looked up at me. "You know what the younger generation is missing?" She paused. "Tears. In my day, when you went to a Bette Davis picture, you cried. When you watched Helen Hayes, you cried. It was heaven. Every Saturday afternoon you could choose your poison. Then the following week you'd rush back to the theater to see it again just for the glorious luxury of crying. Today's audiences don't get to experience this. All they see is shock and *shlock,* I call it. There really are no three-Kleenex movies anymore. Audiences *need* to be touched, to feel, to cry their hearts out once in a while … Oh, listen to me go on." She turned to me. "When are you here next?"

She's inviting me to visit again! "I could come at Christmastime," I answered quickly.

"Perfect. I want you to meet Debbie. You two are kindred spirits. We'll have lunch at the Polo Lounge. In fact, we'll do it a couple of times." Ann smiled. "And with three of us, we won't have to say we've lost someone at the far turn."

Chuckling, I checked the time. It was getting late, and I really needed to hit the road. Then suddenly I remembered the copies of my book that Ann had asked me to bring for her. I excused myself and dashed out to my car to get them. She was happy that I remembered. Back inside I signed them with my new flashlight pen. When I finished, Ann set the MGM book in her lap. The charms on her bracelet jingled as she inscribed it:

For dearest Phillip — you deserve only the best, and these pages provide that. Hurry back. Next time you're here, the two of us will go dancing in the streets.

Love,

Ann

"Would you please sign these, too?" I asked, handing her the egg cartons.

"I've never signed egg cartons before," she said with delight.

While Ann wrote her name on the cartons, I flipped through the pages of my new book. I could tell I was going to love it.

"I never asked you," I said. "How many years were you at the studio?"

"Five in all. From '37 to '42."

"Why did you leave?"

"Believe me, I didn't want to."

"What happened?"

"I was sold down the river."

Seven Sweethearts

*I*t was 1942. Wartime. I'd been entertaining the soldiers at a bond rally at the Great Lakes Naval Station near Chicago. I stood on stage and answered questions. Since I didn't sing and I didn't dance, all I could do was talk. In between shows, we let the officers' wives and their children come backstage. During the intermission, one little boy was climbing me like a tree. His mother said, "You should be flattered. Alvin got out of his sickbed to come see you." I said, "Well, I hope it isn't anything serious."

When I got home, I discovered that MGM had a new producer named Joe Pasternak on trial from Universal. Mr. Pasternak was going to make a picture called Seven Sweethearts *with Kathryn Grayson. When I looked at the script, I did something that I'd never done before. I counted the lines. I had seventeen of them! And they consisted of "Yes," "No," and "Uh, huh." That's when I understood what Mr. Mayer meant by a nothing part. I felt like the seventh sweetheart! Up until then I'd never complained about anything, but I was not happy. So, I marched over to the casting director and said, "Doggone it. I'm doing very well. I've just made* Gone With the Wind *and* Pride and Prejudice. *This is a nothing part."*

"I know. I know," he said, "but Pasternak has to get used to being at a big studio."

"Well, I wish he didn't have to get used to it through me."

The next morning, when I was supposed to begin work on the picture, I woke up looking like a beached frog. My face was swollen, and I couldn't lift my head off the pillow. There was no way I could go to work like that. My mother called the studio and told them, but they didn't believe it. So they sent out a doctor who ascertained that I indeed had the pip. Thanks to Alvin, I had the German measles.

Well, right around that time Darryl Zanuck at Fox had been shooting Orchestra Wives *with Glenn Miller and didn't like what he saw. Zanuck didn't think the leading lady looked innocent enough. So, he contacted Mr. Mayer to see if he could borrow me. When I called in sick, Mr. Mayer thought I was faking it so that I wouldn't have to do the picture. Mayer was already ticked off with me. Around that time, I had asked him if I could be removed from the Hardy pictures. I felt stuck and wanted to do other roles. Laraine Day tried the same tactic to get out of the Dr. Kildare series. Mr. Mayer was furious with me and called me ungrateful. So when Zanuck called him, he said, "I'll sell her to you." When I found out, I felt like a slave.*

Good-bye

I do wish I could tell you my age, but it's impossible. It keeps changing all the time.

— *Greer Garson*

Ann gave me a smirk. "But it turned out to bite Mr. Mayer in the foot. When he let me go, he didn't realize that he needed me for the next Skelton picture. He had to borrow me back for six weeks. Zanuck demanded top dollar, which further infuriated him."

When Ann got the script for *Orchestra Wives*, she was pleased to learn that her leading man was George Montgomery. She'd been on a couple of dates with him and found him fun. "And," she said, "he was gorgeous — one of the handsomest men on the face of the earth." Ann grinned. "And I really liked kissing him. George was a very good kisser." He told Ann that she was his favorite leading lady. Montgomery wound up marrying Dinah Shore, and according to Ann, they had the most beautiful kids you ever saw in your life. After making *Orchestra Wives*, Ann learned that George had been in *The Singing Vagabond* with her back in her Mascot/Republic days. "He never mentioned it," Ann said. "Maybe because he didn't want me to know he was George Letz then."

I asked Ann if she enjoyed making *Orchestra Wives*, and she said,

"Let's just say I wasn't ashamed to be in it. Sometimes you are." Ann loved meeting Glenn Miller and she adored the music. The film featured such songs as "At Last," "Serenade in Blue," and "I've Got A Gal in Kalamazoo," which was nominated for best song at the Academy Awards. "There was a liquid quality to Glen Miller's music," Ann said. "It was soft and memorable and stole its way into your heart. Today, young people miss so much by not having tunes like his to listen to. In my day, you left a theater humming tunes from the picture. What do the young people of today hum on their way home?"

The black dancing team, the Nicholas Brothers, were also featured in *Orchestra Wives*. Ann said, "When word was out on the lot that they were shooting their dance routine and running up the walls, the soundstage was packed. You couldn't have squeezed a sardine on that stage." Ann recalled that because they were black, one of the producers wanted to cut the part where the brothers sang, "I've Got A Gal in Kalamazoo," but Zanuck refused. "You aren't going to cut *anything* with the Nicholas Brothers!" Zanuck exclaimed. He was in their corner.

Ann's first meeting with Zanuck was not what she expected. When she walked into his office, Zanuck shut the door and started chasing her around the room. He was known to be a wolf with the ladies. Well, Ann wanted nothing to do with that, but she didn't want to make an enemy of the man who owned her contract either. She had to quickly think of some way to get out of that sticky situation. She couldn't slap the guy, though she wanted to. So, she started to laugh. "Now stop this at once, Mr. Zanuck," she said, chortling. "You're making me laugh so hard that I can't … I can't breathe." Thrown by Ann's sudden laughing attack and inability to catch her breath, Zanuck stopped. After that, he never chased her around his desk again. But, Ann said it might well have harmed her in the end. Zanuck did nothing for her career. He either threw her into B pictures or loaned her out.

Ann's awkward visit with Zanuck wasn't her first such encounter with a studio executive. At Metro, L.B. Mayer used to invite groups of young starlets up to his office to have "chats" about their careers. Ann went to a couple of them. At one of these meetings, Mr. Mayer invited Ann to sit on his lap. She politely declined. According to Ann, many of the starlets got married as quickly as possible to prevent the "dirty old guys" from chasing them. Apparently, the code of honor said they couldn't run around with married women.

Ann soon grew to hate being at Fox. "It was as cold as a fish," she said. Ann didn't know anybody there and didn't want to. Zanuck, she claimed, didn't respect women. He fought with Janet Gaynor then fired her. He quarreled with Loretta Young, and she left. The same happened to Betty Grable. Ann missed MGM. "There was a quality about it that was so special," she said. "They treated their people so perfectly. And then to go to a place like Fox, where you don't know anybody, and they don't know you — it was not a happy time. So what did I do? I got married!" Zanuck was not happy about it. He liked his stars to remain single so that the studio could manufacture news about their personal lives. Later, Zanuck put Ann in *Bermuda Mystery*, which Ann called a "real stinker." Ann was sure he did that just to get her angry enough to quit. And she did.

Ann Rutherford and George Montgomery in *Orchestra Wives* (1942)
— photo courtesy of the private collection of Miss Rutherford

Bermuda Mystery was one of several film noir pictures Ann made in the '40s. Others included *Inside Job* at Universal, *The Madonna's Secret* at Republic, and *Two O'Clock Courage* at RKO. About the genre, Ann said, "I loved working with all the actors in those pictures with their glorious ugly faces. I also like pictures where men wear hats and start drinking at ten o'clock in the morning." It was during the filming of *Two O'Clock Courage* that Ann was introduced to her future husband Bill Dozier.

As Ann handed me back the egg cartons, she said, "Phil, do you have a warm coat over in Budapest?"

"Funny you should ask that," I said. "I don't, really. Just yesterday, I was at the store looking at some. Why?"

"Well, not long before Bill passed away, he had a coat made in London. He never got to wear it much." My heart clenched. *She's not planning to give me her husband's coat.* Ann pointed to the front of the house. "If you go around the corner, you'll see a closet opposite the powder room." *She is.*

I walked to the closet and opened the door. There in the dark hung a long, green tweed coat. It was the only piece of clothing in the closet. When I took it off the hanger, I spotted the Burberry label stitched on the lining. I carried the coat back to Ann.

"Ah, yes," she said, happy to see it. "That's it." Then she pushed herself up from the chair, set down her cane, and took the coat from my hands. "Let's see if it fits, shall we?" I turned around and put my arms out. Shakily, Ann slid one sleeve over my arm, then another. When I turned back and faced her, she was smiling. "Yes," she said, "I thought it would fit. It looks like it was made for you." Ann straightened the collar and patted my shoulders. "Now you'll be good and warm in Budapest. You gotta be warm."

"I will cherish it," I said, looking down at the coat. "You know I'm never taking this off." I grabbed my things. Then together we walked to the front door and hugged good-bye. "I will call you soon."

"All right," she said with a grin. "You can call me *soon*. You can call me anything you want." I opened the front door, and Ann gave me one last Greer-Dear hug. "Now, Phil, I want you to promise me something. You keep writing, you hear." I promised I would.

Ann stood in the doorway and watched me get into my car. As I started pulling out of the driveway, she motioned for me to roll down the window. I lowered it and stretched over the seat to hear her.

"I love you!" she called out.

I melted. "I love you, too!"

***

I wore the coat on the plane the whole way back to Budapest. During the flight, I replayed Ann's and my conversations in my head. The memory of our visit, like the coat I was wearing, warmed me up. Ann was truly the most fascinating woman I had ever met. "I've been blessed with a full and most fortunate life," she once said to me, "and the fact that I'm allowed to stay on this long is another part of the wonder that I feel about my life."

Though Ann devoted much of her life to the classic era of Hollywood, she lived in the present. She was always going out, sometimes three or four times a week. As she liked to say, "God won't hit a moving target." Ann's views were conservative (she usually voted Republican), but she was open-minded. As a voting member of the Academy, she watched all the nominated films. When she viewed the provocative *The Kids Are All Right* with Julianne Moore and Annette Bening, her older girlfriends were shocked, but Ann thought it was wonderful.

To me, Ann was so much more than a movie star. I wanted to live like her — to put others first, to go after my dreams the way she had, to put my best foot forward, to not squander time. I wanted to be the kind of person who brings people little goodies, buys the neighbor kids special chocolates for Halloween, celebrates with extra ice cream, runs amok once in a while, jumps on a train for a spontaneous trip, and hands out two-dollar bills. I wanted to embrace life like she did and beat others to the hug. Life lessons from my movie star.

When I got back to Budapest, I watched several of Ann's films: *Pride and Prejudice*, a Skelton picture, *Orchestra Wives*, a few with Andy Hardy, and *Gone With the Wind*. As I watched *The Wind*, I kept wondering where Ann was hiding behind the camera.

A couple of weeks later, I gave Ann a call for her birthday. It was early November.

"Hello?" she said, picking up.

"Hi, Ann. It's Phil."

"Who?"

I spoke louder. "Phil Done from Budapest."

"Oh, hello dear." Her voice sounded tired.

"Happy birthday," I said.

"Thanks. I need one like I need a hole in my head."

I laughed. "How are you?"

"Oh," she sighed. "I'm getting better."

"Getting *better*? Is anything wrong?"

"Well, honey, I distinguished myself. I went to a big hoo-ha at the Gene Autry Museum. It was one of those huge affairs under a tent with dinner and entertainment. After dessert, I got up to leave. Well, as soon as I stepped outside, I fell flat on my face."

"Oh, no! Are you OK?"

"Yes, I'm fine, but some blabbermouth called 911, and I wound up at some obscure hospital in Burbank."

Later, I learned from a friend who was with Ann that evening that she had passed out. Fortunately, an ambulance was parked right across the street from the tent. They loaded Ann into the ambulance and gave her oxygen. Ann's good friend Anne Jeffreys rode with her to the emergency room. After Ann came to and stabilized, they moved her to a private room. When Ann's daughter Gloria went to the hospital, she couldn't find her. Anne Jeffreys had registered Ann under a false name to keep the reporters at bay. Ann stayed at the hospital ten days.

"The doctors don't want you to leave," Ann said. "They just want to take their tests. Well, they discovered … I don't know an aorta from a vein, but there is an aorta that goes up through your chest to your heart, and mine isn't behaving. It has a narrow place. It isn't getting enough good stuff through to my heart. Anyway, that's what they found out. First, they scared the living lights out of me. They said, 'We'll have to do open heart surgery.' I said, 'I don't think so.' That scares you. I said, 'Go back and come again.' So, after still more tests, they found that they could replace this one aorta. As I understand it, they just give you a Valium or something, and you can drift off to sleep while they put some device in. They don't even make a hole in your chest. Isn't it fascinating what they can do?" Ann paused. "Oh, I hate all this stuff. I pretend it's not happening. These dang doctor visits are gobbling up all my time."

"Well," I said, trying to cheer her up, "you sound good."

"I *feel* fine. I have no pain whatsoever — except for a big pain in my neck from being told what to do. But the good news is that I'm not anemic anymore. My doctor was stunned when he looked at the numbers."

"How did you accomplish that?"

"I just had a good talk with my veins."

I gave a laugh. "What are you going to do for Thanksgiving?"

"I'm going to lie. I've been invited to three people's homes, and I told them all that I made other plans. I want to do what *I* want to do, to have one full day when I can do anything that comes to my mind. I'm short of time, as it is."

I didn't like hearing that.

"Everyone loves the coat you gave me," I said, switching the subject. "I told everybody about our visit. You're famous in Budapest."

"Oh, aren't you sweet."

"Where are you sitting right now?" I asked. "I want to picture where you are."

"In the kitchen."

"Oh, I never saw it."

"It's a good thing. At this very moment, it's a big mess. I just made myself a big pot of peanut butter soup."

"Peanut butter soup?" I'd never heard of it.

"Oh, it's the most wonderful soup in the world," Ann said. "I know it sounds funny, but it's unbelievable. Next time you're here, I'll make you some. First, you simmer some onions and celery in butter. Then you pour in chicken stock and whisk in about two cups of peanut butter and some cream. Once that's all warm and creamy, you top it with chopped peanuts. It's divine."

Ann told me about a friend of hers back in Vermont who owned a little restaurant. A few years earlier it had come upon hard times. Ann's friend was even thinking of closing the place. One day when the two were on the phone, Ann said, "I'm sending you my recipe for peanut butter soup." Ann mailed it to her, and her friend started making it. Pretty soon, the customers started pouring in with their mugs and thermoses. All they wanted was peanut butter soup.

"The shop hasn't stopped making it since I sent the recipe," Ann said.

"It sounds like the title of a TV movie," I said, smiling. "*Miss O'Hara's Peanut Butter Soup.*"

Ann laughed with me.

I told Ann that I'd been watching several of her pictures and asked if the two of us could watch one or two together the next time I visited.

"That would be wonderful," Ann said. "So long as it's not the last one I made at Metro — *They Only Kill Their Masters*. We made it in 1972. After I saw it, I vowed I'd never look at it again. I called my mother and forbade her to see it, too. I looked like Frankenstein in that picture. The lighting was like what you'd find in a gas station toilet at 3:00 a.m."

A producer friend of Ann's had twisted her arm to make it. Before they started shooting, Ann went to Metro to sign her contract. She hadn't set foot on the lot since the early forties. "When do I go to wardrobe?" she asked a junior assistant, whom she said didn't look old enough to drive. "Wardrobe?" he said. "It's been empty for years." That broke Ann's heart. "Well," Ann said, "I better go check in with the makeup department." He said that was gone, too. They'd do her makeup on the set. Aghast, Ann said, "You mean I have to sit out in front of God and everybody at one of those tacky dressing tables with the cheap light bulbs around it — the kind that the dress extras use?" Then Ann asked what time she needed to report to the set, and the man said seven-thirty. They'd start shooting at eight. "Eight!" Ann cried. "I don't even get dressed to go to the market in half an hour."

On her first day back at Metro, a banner saying, *Welcome Home, Polly Benedict* flew over the main gate. Someone had dug out one of Andy Hardy's old cars, too. The studio also gave the employees on the lot forty-five minutes to make a crowd for Ann. She was touched. Still, the whole experience was not a sentimental affair. Except for a few old photographers and PR guys, almost everybody Ann had known was gone. At lunchtime, she headed over to the commissary to have a bowl of Mr. Mayer's matzo ball soup. When she ordered it, the young woman behind the counter said, "Who's Mr. Mayer?" Ann couldn't eat.

"Going back was so painful," Ann said. "But the hardest blow was walking around the lot. The studio was a mere shadow of what it had once been. I couldn't believe it was the same place. And it was all so eerily still. Ours was the only picture shooting on the lot. Everywhere

I went there was desolation. My beloved wardrobe department was an empty shell, nothing but naked iron racks and forlorn wire hangers. Everything had been sold in the auction. What they didn't sell they threw away. Adrian's once glorious salon was musty, and the deco couches were stained. New England Street, where we shot the picture, had fallen into complete disrepair. They hadn't painted the buildings in decades. They didn't even mow the lawns anymore." Ann paused for a sigh. "I guess I'm becoming like that old back lot. I'm falling into disrepair, too."

"Don't say that," I said. I got off the subject. "I can't wait to see you again."

"You too, honey. Phillip, when you come out here, there's something I want to talk to you about — for the future."

For the future? What could she mean? All I could get out was "OK."

Soon we said our good-byes, and I promised to call. That night, I lay in bed wide awake. What in the world did she want to talk with me about? My mind kept going back to one thing. Maybe Paul was right after all. Maybe Ann Rutherford had found her writer.

Ann Rutherford in 1978
— photo courtesy of the private collection of Miss Rutherford

Hospital

They say the movies should be more like life. I think life should
be more like the movies.

— *Myrna Loy*

Over the next couple of weeks, I called Ann's home several times,
but could never reach her. I was always connected to her
answering service, where a pleasant woman who called me *darlin'*
would take my name and information. She told me that Ann hadn't
been checking her messages. Worried, I continued to call back, but
kept getting the same woman at the service. Then one day a different
woman answered.

"Hello," the voice said.

"Hello," I said. "Ann?"

"No. This is her daughter, Gloria."

"Oh, hello." I introduced myself.

"Yes, I know who you are," she said. "My mother has talked about
you. In fact, she had me go out and buy a couple of your books for
her friends."

I knew about Gloria, too. Ann had spoken about her several
times. Gloria named her cat Clark Gable because he was tall,
adventurous, and gorgeous. Ann had told me about a day many years
before when she came home and found Gloria, who was in grade

school, sulking on the stairs. Ann had retired from films. Ann asked Gloria what was wrong, and she said, "Everybody in my classroom has parents who are somebody, and you're nobody." Ann said, "What are you talking about?" Gloria started listing the kids whose mothers were in movies or television. Ann sat down beside her and said, "I used to be somebody." Gloria didn't believe her. After that, Ann started doing television so she could be "somebody" again.

When Ann first started in television, it was all done live. "It was never dull," Ann said. "You could open a door, and the doorknob would come off, but you had to just continue on, holding the doorknob through the whole scene." In one show, Ann was sitting on the set in a restaurant scene when some guy up in the rafters accidentally hit a bag of artificial snow. It started snowing in the middle of the restaurant, but Ann just kept on going. *

"Is your mother all right?" I asked Gloria.

"She's in the hospital. She had a procedure on her heart. Did she tell you about that?"

"Yes. How is she?"

"She's ..." Gloria paused. "... very weak."

"When will she be able to leave?"

"It's way too early to tell. It could be a couple of weeks, maybe more. We really don't know. All she says is she wants to go home. She tried to sneak out twice already."

I gave a laugh.

"Do you know who Victor is?" Gloria asked.

"Yes."

"The other day she borrowed twenty bucks from him so she could

---

* In the '50s and '60s, Ann performed in such television shows as *Playhouse 90, Climax!, The Donna Reed Show,* and *Perry Mason.* In the '70s, she appeared as Suzanne Pleshette's mother in *The Bob Newhart Show.* Ann got the role because she looked similar to Pleshette.

pay a cab to get out of there."

I laughed again. "May I call her? I'd like to wish her a Merry Christmas."

"We're not really doing Christmas this year. In fact, we're just lucky she's here this Christmas."

I was shocked. Ann made it sound like it would be a simple procedure and that she'd be in and out. "But she's getting better, isn't she?"

Gloria didn't answer. "I'm sure she'd love hearing from you. But I should warn you that she gets mixed up sometimes. And she makes the place sound like the old *Snake Pit* movie, so please take the tales of manhandling with a giant grain of salt. The nurses are lovely, but from my mother's perspective, helping her out of bed is manhandling."

Gloria gave me the name of the hospital and Ann's room number. I thanked her, then called Ann right away.

"Ann, it's Phil."

"Oh, hello dear." It was good to hear her voice.

"I just spoke with Gloria. Are you OK?"

"Yes, I'm fine, but I hate it here. I can't sleep, and the nurses are always coming in and poking and fussing. I think I'm going to have to give everyone a speech."

I was happy to hear that she still had her spunk. Ann and I talked for a few minutes until the nurses came in. Then she had to go.

The following week, I called Ann's home number. I was hoping she might be there already. Again, Gloria answered. She said her mother had been moved to a rehabilitative center. I considered that a good sign. Earlier that day, Ann had walked about fifty feet with a walker and squeezed the ball between her knees, but she didn't like any of it. "She tires easily," Gloria said. "I had a chat with her roommate yesterday, and she said that whenever my mother is on the phone she is so entertaining and animated, but as soon as she hangs up, she's exhausted. My mother, of course, hates the food there. She has a little fridge in her room, so Victor brings her soup every day."

"Peanut butter soup?" I asked.

"As a matter of fact, yes."

"How long do you think she'll be there?"

"Several weeks at least, though we don't tell her that. If she had a full staff at the house, we could bring her home sooner. But I know good and well that the minute I walk out the door, she'll fire everyone, then march downstairs and make herself some scrambled eggs. Even as weak and as fragile as she is now, you have to be very sharp to stay ahead of my mother."

The Return

Old age is no place for sissies.
— *Bette Davis*

I knew a December trip to California was out of the question. Ann needed time to recuperate. Christmastime came and went. In January, I received an e-mail from Gloria saying that her mother was going home at the end of the month. She would have full-time live-in assistance.

I continued to call Ann about once a week, but kept our chats brief as Gloria had asked me to. Ann was happy to be back home. Initially, I could hear the tiredness in her voice, but each time we talked, she sounded more and more like herself. A couple of times when I called, Ann was asleep, so I spoke with her nurse, Marie. When I asked how Ann was doing, she didn't tell me much. This made sense. Marie didn't know me. One day when Ann and I were on the phone, I asked if could visit during my April break. She'd just started having visitors. Ann said yes, and I was thrilled. We didn't set any particular day or time. We'd work out the details when I arrived in California.

When April break came, I flew to Los Angeles, rented a car, and drove to Paul's, where I'd stay for the week. I called Ann the minute I got there. It was Easter Sunday. Marie picked up and handed the phone to Ann, who wished me a Happy Easter. She knew what day it was. A good sign. Ann invited me to come over the following afternoon. I asked if she needed anything, and she said, "No, honey. Just bring your happy self."

That evening, I wrote a list of questions for Ann about her life and career. If she brought up my writing her memoir, I wanted to be ready. Perhaps we could start working on it immediately. I also brought along the DVDs of her films to watch together. If all went well, we could continue working on the project over the phone after I returned to Budapest. As soon as school let out, I could fly back to Beverly Hills in June, and we could work together all summer. I was excited.

The next day, I stopped at the florist on the way to Ann's, bought a hydrangea, and had it wrapped in cellophane. When I arrived at her house, I walked up to the blue door and knocked. No one answered. *This is strange.* It was two. I stepped around to the side yard where her car was parked, but there was no sign of life. Perhaps she's at the doctor's, I thought, or maybe she's running late. I waited for about a half hour on the front step, but no one came. As I walked back to my car, I picked up a golf ball on the lawn. It was good enough for the dentist.

The day, however, was not lost. Later that afternoon, I went to see Al. Before I left Budapest, I had contacted him and made an appointment to get together. He remembered our first meeting when we swapped seats at the Roosevelt Hotel. If Ann agreed to my writing her biography, I wanted to interview Al as well. He'd surely have lots to say. I wasn't going to mention the project to him, though, until I spoke with Ann first.

Al lived in a 1920s stucco bungalow in West Hollywood, just off the main street. He greeted me with a smile as he opened the door.

He was more stooped over than I remembered. Just a few white hairs remained on his shiny head. I figured he had to be close to Ann's age. As Al gave me a tour of his home, he told me that he'd moved out from Indiana in the '50s after finishing his service. When I asked why he chose California, he put his hands up like a scale and tossed me an isn't-it-obvious sort of look. "Let's see — Indianapolis or Hollywood?" He laughed, and I laughed along with him.

A black Steinway grand filled the corner of the living room. Al was a musician. For years, he'd played in clubs all over Los Angeles. At one time, he also owned a movie memorabilia shop on Santa Monica Boulevard where he sold posters, lobby cards, and stars' autographs. Al had a clever way of acquiring autographs. If an actor had sung in a movie, instead of handing them a photo to sign, he presented a piece of music from the film. They'd be so tickled to see the music that they always signed it.

Once, when Al was working in a Hollywood box office, he spotted Cary Grant's name on the reservations list. The next day, Al brought a piece of sheet music titled "Suzy" to the theater. Cary had sung it in the picture by the same name. On the night of the show, Grant stepped up to the ticket window and asked how much the ticket was even though he knew there would be no charge. Stars never paid for their tickets; places were just so happy to have them there. Smiling, Al pulled out the music and said, "Your payment will be to autograph this." Cary laughed when he saw it. "Well, I better sign it quick," he said. "The other two on the cover are dead." Grant put both hands on the counter and said, "You know, these aren't the original lyrics. I sang different ones in the movie." Then right there at the window, Cary sang the original lyrics. Al beamed at the memory. "Cary Grant sang to me!"

The top of Al's piano was covered with stacks of music and several framed photographs of Al and Ann with stars from Hollywood's golden age: Kathryn Grayson, Debbie Reynolds, Jane Powell, Esther Williams, Cyd Charisse, Marsha Hunt, Joan Leslie. Al said that most of the women, if they were still around, were pretty frail now. In all the photos, the ladies were beautifully dressed. Al said that whenever any of them stepped outside of their own front doors, they were always "meticulously turned out." Studio training had been ingrained in their very beings. Every couple of years, a group of them got together for lunch. Al was allowed to join them because he was the driver. Most, like Ann, had started in pictures in their teens. Ann called them her sorority sisters. MGM was their university. "Even though they're in their golden years," Al said, "when they reminisce about the old days, they all still refer to L. B. Mayer as Mr. Mayer." Al smiled. "Old habits die hard."

In one of the photos, Ann was standing with Ann Miller, whom everyone called Annie. The two had been good friends. They were known as the two Anns. Then when they started palling around with Anne Jeffreys of *Topper* fame, it became the three Anns. Ann Rutherford liked to tease Anne Jeffreys about the dangling *e* in her first name.

One Easter weekend, Al turned on the television, and there was Annie Miller dancing in *Easter Parade* with Fred Astaire. He rang her and said, "Hey, I'm watching you on TV." The next morning, Al woke up, switched the set on again, and there was Annie, dancing the same number. Al called her back up and said, "My God! I just turned on the television, and you're *still* dancing!"

Al said he could have filled a book with Annie Miller's one-liners. One day during the war, she and Ann Rutherford were visiting a veterans' hospital together when they stopped to talk with a soldier who had lost a leg. Annie patted his shoulder and said, "Better luck next time."

Al's favorite Annie Miller story took place when she was doing *Sugar Babies* on Broadway with Mickey Rooney. Every week after the Sunday matinee, Annie would fly to California to see her mother. She didn't perform on Mondays. Then she'd fly back to New York in time for the Tuesday evening show. Once after she got back to New York, Annie realized that she'd left her phone book at her mother's. So, she called her mom and asked her to mail it. Her mother said sure and put it in the mail. She mailed her the Los Angeles telephone book.

When Annie passed away, Al and Ann attended her funeral together. At the service, the MC announced, "Let's give Annie what she always wanted, shall we?" Everyone stood up and gave her a standing ovation.

As Al and I stood at the piano, he picked up one of the photos and wiped the glass with his shirt. In it, Ann Rutherford was standing with Natalie Wood. "Do you know about their connection?" he asked. "Ann's very proud of that."

In 1943, Ann was on location in Santa Rosa filming *Happy Land* for Fox. Her mother was with her. Ann needed an outside dressing room, so the studio rented a small, teardrop trailer from a young family in the area. The woman who owned the trailer came to the set every day to clean it. She'd bring her four-year-old daughter along. Ann and her mother thought the child was adorable, one of the cutest kids they'd ever seen.

One day, Ann asked the director, Irving Pichel, if he could somehow put the little girl in the picture. Ann was sure the family could use the money. There was a scene coming up where people step into a drugstore. Ann suggested that someone walk in holding the little girl's hand. Pichel said, "Oh, sure. She's a cute kid." And the girl got a couple of days' work out of it.

A few years later, Ann's phone rang at home. It was Pichel. He was getting ready to make *Tomorrow is Forever* with Claudette Colbert and Orson Welles. "What was the name of that family in Santa Rosa with that cute little girl?" he asked. Ann couldn't remember, so she rang her mother. "Gurdin," her mother said. "And the little girl was Natasha." They were Russian. Ann called Pichel back and gave him the child's name. Little Natasha, with her new name of Natalie Wood, got the part. Only one year later, she would make the classic *Miracle on 34th Street* and become one of the top child stars in Hollywood. Thanks to Ann Rutherford.

Upstairs

Now I know I have a heart — because it's breaking.
        — The Tin Man, *The Wizard of Oz*

Al and I walked to a restaurant on the main street where we sat outside and ordered iced teas. As we waited for our drinks, he told me about when he first met Ann.

A man named Steve came into Al's shop one day and said, "Do you have any Ann Rutherford?" He wanted everything Al had. Steve said he was going to an autograph signing that Ann would be attending and asked if Al wanted to come along. The two of them went, and that's where Al and Ann met. Later, Steve and Al phoned Ann and asked her out to dinner. Ann said, "Well … I don't know you, so I don't think we should go to dinner. But we can do lunch." Steve and Al took Ann to the Polo Lounge, not knowing Ann loved the place so much, and hit it off.

"Did you have Bloody Marys?" I asked, smiling.

He paused to think about it. "I think we did."

Al and I started talking about the *Gone With the Wind* festivals that he attended with Ann. He told me that at the events Ann would sit and sign autographs for hours at a time. She knew that people came to see her and that some traveled long distances, so she would never take a break. In twenty years, Al said he'd only seen Ann use the ladies' room once. He called her The Camel of Beverly Hills. When Ann would get tired at the signings, she'd have to concentrate on getting her signature right. She'd say out loud, "One loop, two loops, three loops, four." There were four loops in the way she wrote "Rutherford." Friends who were with her would say, "Ann, you're getting loopy," and she would laugh.

"Her autograph isn't worth a dime anymore," Al said. "She's given too many. The volunteers who assist her are told to keep her fans moving because otherwise she would talk to each one forever. I remember at one signing, I was sitting beside Ann when she started talking to a fan about her career. She began at 1933 when she was in radio. I turned away. When I turned back ten minutes later, I thought — my God! She's only on *1936!*"

"Are you two planning to go to any *Gone With the Wind* events this year?" I asked.

Al slunk back in his chair. His smile had disappeared. "She won't go out again. We're done."

It was hard to hear that.

Al and I finished our drinks then walked back to his place. He didn't say much on the way home. I was sure he was thinking of Ann. Back at his house, he sat down at the piano and started playing "Someone to Watch Over Me." As his old fingers moved effortlessly over the keys, he started talking. "Ann has a theory about melody," he said. "Melody, she says, is something we all need, something every person longs for. When rock came along, suddenly you couldn't hear a decent melody on the radio. Noise and beat just wiped everything off the air. According to Ann, the world started falling apart when melody disappeared from our lives." As Al continued to play, he sang the last few bars of the song. His old voice was no longer able to hold the notes. When he finished, his eyes were moist. At that moment, I saw how much he loved his dear friend. Ann was his melody.

Al stood up and regained his smile. Then, without telling me where we were going, he led me out to the garage behind his house, unlocked the door, and lifted it. Inside, hundreds of old movie posters, leftovers from his store, leaned against the walls. Excited, I asked if he had anything from Ann's pictures. "I think so," he said. "I've sold so much." Then he started thumbing through his collection and opened a few file cabinets packed with sheet music and memorabilia. "Here you go," he said, pulling out a lobby card. It was of Ann and Mickey in *Andy Hardy Meets Debutante*. Ann had signed it. I offered to buy the card, but Al refused. "It's yours," he said. "But that autograph isn't worth a nickel."

When I called Ann's the next morning, the nurse answered and gave her the phone. I didn't say anything about our missed visit. Again, Ann said to come over around two. Finally, I would see her. I'd started to worry that I wasn't going to get the chance. That afternoon, I drove to Greenway Drive. With the hydrangea in hand and my questions and DVDs in my bag, I walked up to the front door and rang the doorbell.

"Who is it?" a voice called out. It had to be Marie.

"It's Phil Done," I said through the door. "Ann's friend. We've spoken on the phone a couple of times. Ann told me to come by at two."

The lock clicked, and the door opened halfway. A short black woman in a nurse's smock peeked around the door.

"Are you Marie?" I asked.

"Yes. Miss Rutherford didn't tell me you were coming."

Uh oh. For a moment, Marie stared at me. I could tell that she was deciding whether or not to let me in. *Oh, God. I hope she doesn't turn me away. I've traveled so far.* I held out the flowers. "These are for Ann." The door opened, and Marie invited me in. Relieved, I stepped inside.

The entryway was tidier than the last time I'd seen it. The stacks of fan mail were gone from the tables and chairs. I commented on how nice everything looked. Marie said that Gloria and Ann's grandsons had cleaned the whole place.

"Why don't you wait here," Marie said, "and I'll go upstairs and tell her you're here." As Marie started up the stairs, I asked how Ann was. Marie paused before answering. "She has good days and bad days."

While I waited in the entry, I smiled at the double-handled bucket and the pain-to-dust chandelier. It felt good to be in the house again. I could hear Marie speaking, but couldn't make out the words. Soon she leaned over the banister and called down. "You may come up. Miss Rutherford didn't recall that she told you to come." My heart sank. Ann hadn't remembered.

I walked up the staircase, and Marie pointed me to a bedroom door. Entering the room, I was not prepared for what I saw.

For a second, I couldn't believe it was really Ann. It hardly looked like her. Wrapped in a blue bathrobe, Ann lay in a chrome hospital bed. She looked like she'd melted into the bedclothes. Her face was gaunt, her mouth open.

As I stepped over to the bed, I forced a smile. "Hello," I said, trying to hide my shock.

Ann didn't respond.

I leaned over to kiss her cheek, and Ann turned her head slightly. It took effort. Her brown eyes stared at me intently from behind her thick glasses. It looked as though she was trying to figure out who I was.

"I brought you flowers," I said, ignoring the knot in my throat. I set them on a table at the foot of the bed.

"They're ..." I leaned in closer to hear her. It was hard for her to get the words out. "... they're beautiful."

Marie entered the room and offered to take the hydrangea. As she picked it up, Ann called out, "I'm not receiving today." Her voice sounded desperate. The words crushed my heart like a vise. *She doesn't want to see me.* Then I corrected myself. *No, Phil. That's not true. She doesn't want me to see her this way.*

For a few long moments, Ann and I sat in silence. I couldn't think of anything to say. Looking around the room, I figured it was probably her daughter's. It was too small to be Ann's. A couple of Easter baskets and bouquets with get-well cards sat on the nightstands. The sun spilled through a window opposite the bed. Propped up on a club chair in the corner of the room sat a stuffed Mickey Mouse doll. I wondered if it was the one from Walt Disney. I wanted to ask Ann about it, but didn't. It may have confused her. I remembered what Ann said about *Gone With the Wind* being like Mickey Mouse.

"What a nice room," I said, trying to sound upbeat.

Ann said something, but I didn't understand. Her tongue got in the way.

"The house looks great downstairs," I reported.

"It better!" she shot out.

I brightened. *There she is. There's that sparkle.*

"I saw Al yesterday," I said.

Slowly, Ann turned her head toward me. "He's a nice man," she said, flatly. The sparkle had already left.

"Yes," I said. "We talked about Ann Miller and Natalie Wood. I didn't realize you discovered her."

Ann didn't answer.

I put my hand on Ann's and held it. Her skin was cold. After a few moments, Marie poked her head into the room. This was my sign to leave. I leaned over Ann with the largest smile I could muster. "Well," I said, "I just dropped by to say hello."

"I appreciate it," she said, her voice trailing off.

Then I stood up and kissed her cheek again. I'd flown halfway around the world, and our visit was only a few minutes. Still, I was glad I made the trip. I knew this would be the last time I'd ever see her. As I stood over her, it looked as though she was still trying to figure out who I was. I hoped, for her sake, that she couldn't.

I tucked in the blanket then got up to go. At the doorway, I turned around for one last look. Ann was still staring at me. I pushed another smile, waved, and stepped out of the room.

In the hallway, I leaned over the back of a chair for a few moments. It felt like the wind had been knocked out of me. My lungs didn't want to take my breath. Then, numb, I started walking toward the stairs. I spotted Marie watching television in a large room and stepped in to thank her for letting me see Ann.

"I … I didn't realize that she was so bad," I said, shaking my head. "I just saw her in October, and she was fine."

Marie just pressed her lips together, sympathetically.

"Does she get up?" I asked.

"Yes. I make her. But she doesn't want to."

"Is she eating?"

Marie waited a beat. "We're working on that."

I glanced around the room. The walls were papered with soft green ferns. A canopied, four-poster bed stood in the center. Sunlight slanted through the lace curtains, hitting the thick white carpet and lids of silver-topped jars on the nightstands.

"Is this Ann's room?" I asked.

"Yes."

I asked if I could look around, and Marie nodded. She joined me as I stepped into a large bathroom where perfume bottles with fancy stoppers rested on mirrored trays. The room smelled of lavender sachets and fancy soap. A partially open closet door revealed traveling cases with Ann's initials and long gowns hanging on padded satin hangers. I wondered if any of the sleeves were still stuffed with tissue paper. As I scanned the room, I recalled a scene from David Selznick's *Rebecca* when Joan Fontaine walks around the first Mrs. de Winter's glorious bedroom at Manderley.

Back in the bedroom, a small bookshelf close to Ann's bed caught my eye. On it sat two rows of books, only biographies, nothing else. There must have been well over two dozen of them. I crouched down and looked at the names in the titles: Judy Garland, Debbie Reynolds, Myrna Loy, Ava Gardner, Ann Miller, Esther Williams, Greta Garbo, Rosalind Russell, even Joan Crawford. Ann's sorority sisters. She'd kept them close.

And then my eye fell upon an object lying on the foot of the chaise. I walked over and looked down at it. It was a faded program from *Gone With the Wind*. Was it hers from the premiere? Had she been looking at it? I wanted to pick it up and see if the backside was blank, but I didn't dare touch it.

"Would you like to see the rest of the house?" Marie asked, breaking my thoughts.

"Yes, please," I answered. I didn't tell her that I'd already seen most of the downstairs.

Marie escorted me to a paneled room down the hall with overstuffed green leather chairs and tall, glass-fronted shelves stuffed with books. Resting on an oak rolltop desk lay a forest green leather desk set and a brass-handled letter opener. Shades with crystal finials topped blue and white porcelain lamps. This must have been her husband's study. It looked like Ann hadn't removed any of his things. Like the coat.

Silently, Marie and I descended the staircase. As we walked through the living room, library, and bar, I tried to take in all the details, absorbing things in a slow, observant manner. Then Marie took me into an area of the house that I hadn't seen before. We moved through the breakfast nook, kitchen, and the formal dining room with its black-and-white tiled floors and hand-painted porcelain plates that hung on the wall. Atop a long, highly polished mahogany dining table sat cardboard boxes of old, black-and-white stills of Ann. It appeared as though her family had already started going through her things.

Marie and I ended in the sunroom, where I spotted the album with Ann's magazine covers. I asked if it would be OK if I looked at it, and Marie said yes. I picked it up and took a seat where Ann and I had sat when I first visited her. As I flipped through the pages, Marie stood over my shoulder. My guess was that she hadn't seen it before.

"She was a beautiful lady," Marie said softly.

"Yes," I said. "She was stunning."

Then Marie shook her head and spoke one word. "Age."

I wanted to stay and pore over the album, but I knew I shouldn't linger. I'd already stayed too long. I stood up and walked with Marie through the entry. Marie could see that the visit had been difficult for me.

"You know something," she said, opening the door, "the first day I started working for Miss Rutherford, she told me that I always needed to come to work with my hair done, my uniform starched, and my face on. I asked her why, and she said, 'Honey, the second I kick the bucket, there will be photographers knocking at my door, and you need to look your best.' "

Ann Rutherford at the Marietta Country Club (2007)
— photo courtesy of Connie Sutherland and Marietta Gone With the
Wind Museum

Ann signs a photo of herself as Carreen O'Hara at the Marietta Gone With
the Wind Museum (2007). She is wearing Madame Butterfly.
— photo courtesy of Marietta Gone With the Wind Museum

Afterword

Come on-a my house.

— *Rosemary Clooney*

Two months later, on June 11, 2012, Ann Rutherford passed away at her home. She was ninety-four. Her dear friend Anne Jeffreys was at her side. I was happy to learn that Ann hadn't left this world alone. After reading the news, I went to my closet, pulled out my Burberry coat, and wrapped myself up in it. Then I lit a candle, placed it on the windowsill, and sat there in the dark till it almost burned out. At Ann's request, no funeral services were held. Ann had often said, "I want people to be happy that they knew me, not gather and be sad that I'm gone."

The next couple of days, I read the online obituaries as they poured in from all over the world. I was surprised, actually, at how many there were. I knew Ann's death would make the news, but I had no idea it would garner such huge press. Most of the major newspapers in the U.S. and the United Kingdom carried the story. Every article mentioned Ann's role in the Hardy pictures and of course *The Wind.* Ann had been right. She'd always said that no matter what else she or the other surviving cast members had done, their obituaries would say they were in the cast of *Gone With the*

Wind.

Friends wrote and called with their condolences. Paul phoned from Santa Monica. He told me that large wreaths of flowers had been placed beside both of Ann's stars on Hollywood Boulevard.

During our conversation, I said, "Well, so much for the book."

"What are you talking about?" he said.

"Paul, she's dead."

"All the more reason to write it."

"But I was going to write it *with* her."

"So, write it yourself. Have you started?"

"Not really. I've made some notes. That's all."

"Contact the people who knew her," Paul said. "They'll help, I'm sure. Phil, you told me the world had to know this woman. So — tell 'em. It will be your tribute. And from what you've told me about Ann Rutherford, I have a feeling she'll be helping you with this."

After I hung up the phone, I thought hard about it. Maybe I *could* do this. I turned on the computer. Ann's photo from a Hardy picture was on my screensaver. She looked like she'd just won an argument with Mickey Rooney. Her chin was raised; the corners of her mouth hinted a smile. Her expression looked as if she were about to say, "… *well?*" I started typing. As I began writing, I recalled the charm bracelet that Ann wore when we went to the Polo Lounge — her life on a wrist. I decided that this was how I would structure the book. Each story, told in Ann's voice, would be a charm on the bracelet of her life.

The first person I reached out to was Anne Jeffreys. She told me about the night that Ann passed away. "The week before she died," Miss Jeffreys said over the phone, "I brought Ann a bottle of Dubonnet wine. It was her favorite. We kept it in the medicine cabinet near her bed. She'd moved to the big bedroom by then. Each time I visited, I pulled out the bottle and poured it into pink plastic champagne glasses. As I did, I'd sing the jingle from the Dubonnet commercial. It made her smile. Ann couldn't sit up, so I'd hold the glass to her lips and pour a little sip into her mouth. We did this a couple of times. Then one night, I could see that she was really slipping. Ann's eyes were closed; she wouldn't open them. Her mouth remained open. She wasn't responding. I had to put my head on her chest to see if she was still breathing. I knew the end was very near. Leaning over her, I whispered, 'Annie dear, I think it's time for Dubonnet. Blink your eyes if it's time for a toast.' I waited. Then, ever so slightly, I could see one eyelid trying to open. I poured the wine into her pink champagne glass and touched it to her lips. And then she was gone."

Miss Jeffreys also told me that a week before Ann passed, she was sitting at her bedside, praying for her friend. Ann's eyes were closed. It appeared that she was asleep. Marie stepped into the room and whispered, "I'm not sure you should bother prayin'. I don't think she's a believer." Ann's eyes popped open. "Who says I'm not a believer?" Then she shut her eyes and said, "Annie, keep prayin'."

After speaking with Miss Jeffreys, I contacted Chris Sullivan, the man to whom Ann gave the locket. Chris described the moment he received it. "It arrived in an ordinary envelope," he explained. "Ann sent it regular mail, not certified. I noticed that the envelope was lumpy. I opened it and pulled out a birthday card. The locket was inside the card, wrapped in tissue paper. There was no other protection. Of course I knew immediately what it was. I confess — I was so moved that I had to give myself a couple of days to call and thank her properly. But before I had the chance, Ann phoned me and asked if I'd received something in the mail." Chris also told me that one night a couple of months after she was given the locket, Ann heard tapping on her bedroom window. She got up to see what was going on. In the front yard stood the groom from the wedding where she'd received the locket. He was throwing pebbles and wanted to come up. Ann opened the window and told him to scram.

Chris, an M.D., said that Ann was proud of the fact that she'd outlived all of her doctors. After Ann's main doctor passed away in the '80s, she never sought out another one until her recent heart trouble. Ann had always been skeptical of doctors. She'd say, "Honey, all they want to do is find something wrong with you." But she trusted Chris. Whenever Ann needed medical advice, she called him. Chris told me that Ann went in for the heart procedure because she had aortic stenosis, a narrowing of the major valve in the heart. He suspected that the reason she deteriorated so quickly after the procedure was that she had some strokes.

Connie Sutherland, director of the Marietta Gone With the Wind Museum, said that Ann was the type of person who would just pick up the phone because she was thinking of you. "She had all my phone numbers," Connie said, "but you never knew which one she was going to use. She had my number at work, but would call my cell; she had my home number, but would call work. She just picked any number and called it."

Both Connie and Chris spoke about how much Ann loved her fans. She loved being approached and fussed over and asked for her autograph. She heard the same comments over and over again: "Oh, I loved you in the Hardy pictures." "*Gone With the Wind* is my favorite movie!" "Oh, you were so pretty!" Still, she responded with absolute delight, as though she had never heard anyone say these things before. At the *Gone With the Wind* festivals, Ann would never charge for her autograph, though it was common practice to do so. "These people paid to come see my movies," she would say. "Why would I charge them now?" If a young person approached Ann at an event, she was known to take them by the hand and say, "Oh, I'm so glad you young people are here. We *need* you. *Gone With the Wind* belongs to you. Protect it and pass it on."

Connie recalled one festival where Robert Osborne of Turner Classic Movies interviewed Ann in front of a large audience. Ann was talking about making *Adventures of Don Juan* with Errol Flynn. Osborne asked if she and Errol ever fooled around. "Well ... I ..." Ann stammered. "We ... I was too busy working to *date*." Osborne grinned. "I never asked you if you dated. I asked if you fooled around." Ann never did really answer the question.

According to Connie, when Ann was alive it never really was clear what her true age was. She'd lied about it for years. Ann absolutely abhorred when an interviewer asked her age. Her stock answer: "I'm an actress. What age would you *like* me to be?" Connie said that Ann would have been horrified that her true age was printed in the *New York Times*. Once, Connie called Chris in a panic. They were making flight arrangements for Ann to come out to Marietta, and the airline demanded to know Ann's exact birthdate. "I'm not going to ask her. *You* ask her!" went back and forth. No one had the nerve to ask. Somehow they worked it out. When Ann told Connie about her heart condition, she said, "Well, dear, after all I *am* ninety-four." Connie knew then that it was serious. It was the first time Ann said how old she really was.

Everyone I spoke with had a favorite Ann story. Ed Faulkner, Ann's second cousin, remembered when Ann and her mother visited his family in Lexington, Kentucky on their way to the Atlanta premiere. Ed was seven years old at the time and in second grade. He took Ann to school for Show and Tell. "I had the biggest chest in the world," Ed said. "The kids were allowed to ask questions, and one asked how much money she made." Friend Joseph Yakovetic recalled a time when he visited Ann at her house. There had been a leak in the upstairs bathroom, and Ann's checkbook had gotten wet. Joseph found her in the sunroom ironing checks.

Fellow MGM contract player Marsha Hunt, with whom Ann made three pictures, visited Ann's home in Northridge about half a dozen times after she married David May. Marsha remembered their butler. "He was a southern black man," Marsha said, "and he answered the phone in a cadence that almost made me want to break into a soft shoe. 'This is Mrs. David May the second's residence,' he sang. It had a beat to it. I used to love to call Ann's place just to hear it." Then Marsha added, "Mrs. David May the *second*. I never thought of Ann as second in anything."

Caren Marsh-Doll, former MGM contractee and one of Judy Garland's stand-ins for *The Wizard of Oz*, said that she and Ann used to double date back in the '30s. "Over the years, Ann and I kept in touch," Caren said. "We'd call each other on the phone, and she always called me Caren Sweetheart. I loved that. At the end of our talks, Ann would always say, 'Honey, just stay vertical.' "

Neighbor Linda Lindsley recalled Ann and Bill's love of dogs. They always had several. Ann's favorite was a white miniature poodle named Sibyll. Ann liked to give her dogs people names. Bill's boxer was Sugar, short for Sugar Ray Leonard. Bill took Sugar to work with him every day. There were periods when Ann and Bill had as many as five or six dogs at one time. In the 1960s, Beverly Hills had a limit of two dogs per home. (Ann would register her dogs with the neighbors.) One day, an inspector from Animal Control was walking door to door and stopped at the Doziers. When he rang the bell, all the dogs went racing to the entry, barking up a storm. Opening the door and seeing the inspector, Ann turned on her best scatterbrained voice and announced, "It's Sibyll's birthday, and all her friends came over to celebrate. We're just about to have some cake. Would you like some cake?" The inspector let it go.

Another friend of Ann's who was friendly with Botox nudged Ann more than once to give it a try. Ann always declined. Then one day, Ann agreed to have an injection in the crease between her eyes. It cost $1,000. Ann was actually pleased with the result, but about two months later, she noticed that the crease reappeared. Ann was furious. She didn't realize that Botox wore off. "What a racket!" Ann cried. "Never again, honey!"

Reporter Bill Ruelman said that out of the hundreds of celebrity interviews he'd conducted, Ann's was the easiest. It took place at the Williamsburg Film Festival. Bill had done his homework and prepared a long list of questions. After introducing Ann, he asked his first one. Ann turned to the audience and began to speak. "She didn't take a breath," Bill said. "After fifteen minutes, I just put my questions down, sat back, and let her talk. Ann went on for a good thirty minutes, at least. Finally, she turned back to me and smiled. 'Honey,' she said, 'did you have a question?' "

Author John Fricke had a similar experience. In 2009, he was interviewing Ann at a festival in Cadiz, Ohio for the shared anniversary of *Gone With the Wind* and *The Wizard of Oz*. There were several hundred people in the audience. "I asked my first question," John said with a chuckle, "and Ann talked for twenty minutes straight. She never drew breath. Everything she said was fascinating, but eventually I had to cut in to let the other guests on the panel share. Ann was apologetic, but the next day we had a second interview in front of another large audience, and she did the whole thing over again." At the end of our conversation, John said that when he thinks of Ann, all the right adjectives come to mind:

gracious, feminine, happy, positive, and classy.

Jackie Autry, Gene Autry's wife, described Ann as beautiful both in and out. "Ann had a demeanor about her that caught everyone's attention," Jackie said. "She had a rich sense of herself and the impact she had on others." Jackie told me that when Ann and Gene would get together, they'd giggle like two teenagers. "I'm sure," Jackie said, "that she and Gene are together again, carrying on as they did in real life."

Jonathan Weedman used to escort Ann to openings of the L.A. Philharmonic and various events. Once he and Ann attended a party held at the Minolta Planetarium. During the evening, the guests could go watch the star show. Ann and John walked into the dark planetarium, sat down in the comfortable chairs, and looked up at the ceiling. Soon, they both nodded off. When they awoke, John turned to Ann and said, "Well at least I can now say that I slept with Ann Rutherford." Ann cracked up.

Jonathan's favorite Ann memory took place at the Avalon theater in Hollywood at an event honoring Tab Hunter. There were about four hundred guests. Right in the middle of the tributes, Ann pushed herself up from her table and cried, "You don't know the half of it!" Everyone was shocked. She wasn't supposed to speak. But no one dared say anything because it was Ann Rutherford. Then Ann hobbled on her cane to the center of the room and proceeded to tell the audience how devotedly Tab and his partner had looked after Evelyn Keyes, Ann's sister in *Gone With the Wind*, in the last years of her life. Nobody had spoken about it during the evening, and Ann wanted everyone to know. When she finished giving her speech, the room applauded, and Ann walked back to her chair. "And *that*," said Jonathan, "was Ann Rutherford."

David Simon, Ann's nephew, recalled walking down the street as a small boy with his mother Judith and Aunt Ann. On more than one occasion, people would come up to them and ask if David was Ann's son. Judith had red hair, and David's was brown like Ann's. It was the family joke that Ann was David's mother.

Anne Jeffreys remembered a cruise the two of them took together. "You couldn't get through the cabin door," Anne Jeffreys said. "Ann had so many shopping bags everywhere." When it was time to go to sleep, the two got into their beds and said good night. Anne Jeffreys grabbed the remote to the television and turned it off. Ann Rutherford bolted up and said, "What are you doing? I can't sleep without the TV on!" Later, when Anne Jeffreys saw that her friend had fallen asleep, she quietly turned off the television. Again, Ann sprang up and cried, "What are you *doing?*" So, the TV stayed on all night — and every night after that. After Anne Jeffreys relayed the story, I told her what Ann Rutherford had told me about her on that same cruise. "I don't know how she does it," Ann had said. "Annie Jeffreys looks just as beautiful sleeping as she does when she goes out for the evening." Anne Jeffreys laughed when she heard it.

Bonnie Strangis, a close friend of the Doziers and Bill's assistant for many years, said that Ann loved to go out to eat. "It could be the seediest place on earth," said Bonnie, "but if they served hot bread, Ann was happy. She loved hot bread." David Simon recalled that one of Ann's favorite restaurants was Hamburger Hamlet on Sunset Boulevard. A few months before she died, David and his family took Ann there. "I'll never forget that evening," David said. "Ann wasn't doing well then. As we were sitting at our table, a couple stepped over to her and said, 'Excuse me. Aren't you Ann Rutherford?' I couldn't believe it. Even at ninety-four and in failing health, they *still* recognized her."

Many described Ann as a gracious hostess. Close friend Rose

Narva said that Ann liked to host luncheons at the Polo Lounge. "She always wanted to arrive early," Rose said. "I'd help put little gifts out on the table for each guest and set the name cards. Very few people do that anymore. It was very old Hollywood." Linda Lindsley fondly remembered parties at Ann's home. "Every detail was just perfect — the table settings, the food. She even put eggshells in the coffee to take the bitterness away." Bonnie Strangis agreed. "Everything had a special touch to it. It didn't matter what the holiday was — Halloween, Easter, Christmas — the house was filled with the most beautiful decorations all made by Ann herself." Both Bonnie and Linda were married at Ann's home. In fact, Ann and Bill hosted several weddings at their house, which Bill jokingly referred to as Greenway Chapel.

David Simon said that when he was growing up, Ann and Bill hosted Thanksgiving. (Ann's sister Judith was in charge of Christmas.) It was always a lavish affair. They'd invite about twenty-five to thirty guests. Half were family, and the other half were people who didn't have any place to go for the holiday. The feast, David said, was always done up like it came right out of *Gone With the Wind*.

In my interviews, Ann's love of jewelry often came up. Ann's stepdaughter, Deborah Dozier Potter, said that her father liked to have jewelry made for Ann, often from Beverly Hills jeweler William Ruser. Ann liked fountains, so Bill had several pins made to look like them. Bill also had a brooch made in the shape of hands because Ann was always doing something with them. One of her slogans was, "Busy hands are happy hands."

Bonnie Strangis said that Ann wore diamonds almost every day. "She never stepped out of the house until she was ready to be seen. She was always camera ready, always a star." Once Ann went to

Bonnie's for a July Fourth barbecue. Ann was decked out in sapphires, rubies, and diamonds — all red, white, and blue. When Bonnie commented on it, Ann said, "It's my Fourth of July jewelry!"

Betty Graham, Bill's former assistant, said Ann didn't believe in theft insurance. Ann once told her, "Anyone who wants to take something from me will have a hard time finding it." Ann whispered to Betty that she sewed her jewels into the hems of her draperies. She told another friend that she hid them in the refrigerator.

David Hayes, Ann's dress designer for many years, recollected that Ann preferred wearing solid color clothes that could show off her jewelry. (According to her stepdaughter, Ann preferred flocked white Christmas trees for the same reason; they showed off her ornaments.) More than once, David asked Ann about a certain piece of jewelry he hadn't seen her wear for a while. Ann would cringe and say, "Well, I took it off and set it in a safe place, but now I can't remember where I put it." After Ann passed away, David was sure that her daughter found jewelry all over the house. Hayes also said that Ann Rutherford and Anne Jeffreys would sometimes wear his matching ensembles to festivals and premieres. They got a kick out of it. Once, when the two Anns walked down a red carpet, they overheard a woman say, "Oh, what a shame. They must be so embarrassed. They arrived in the same outfit."

Ann told Chris Sullivan that she wore Madame Butterfly to bed. Ann kept a large jar of cold cream open on her nightstand. Her plan was that if a burglar broke into her home at night, she'd take Madame Butterfly off and dunk it into the jar to hide it.

Ann Jeffreys recalled an incident with Madame Butterfly when she and Ann were traveling to New York for Liza Minnelli's wedding. At Kennedy Airport, Ann walked through security and set the alarm off. The guard asked if she had anything in her pockets, and Ann said no. She walked through the detector again, and once again the alarm rang. This scene repeated two more times until Ann finally fessed up. She'd pinned Madame Butterfly to the inside of her bra. She wanted to take it to New York, but was afraid that if someone saw it they'd hit her over the head and swipe it.

When Ann fainted at the Gene Autry event, she was wearing a long diamond necklace (Ann bought it for herself after David May passed away) and her wedding ring from David. On the way to the hospital, Anne Jeffreys removed both pieces so they would be safe. Later, when Ann woke up in her hospital bed, she was in a panic because her jewelry was gone. Right around that time, Anne Jeffreys called and explained that she had taken it. Ann told her that she couldn't sleep without her diamond ring. So, Anne Jeffreys drove back to the hospital, and Ann put it on. Together they wrapped gobs of tape around the ring so that no one could steal it while Ann was asleep.

A couple of friends lovingly mentioned Ann's driving. Bill Sasser, director of the Williamsburg Film Festival, recalled the time Ann drove him and a few others around Beverly Hills to see the celebrities' homes. "We visited about fifteen places," Bill said, "but I never saw any of them. Ann would pull up to the front of a house and say, 'Here's Ronnie Reagan's home.' Then she'd pop the accelerator, everyone would go flying back in their seats, and Ann was off to the next place." Friend Larry Floyd had a similar experience. "Ann had just driven me by Randolph Scott's house," Floyd said. "Then she whipped out of the cul-de-sac. I thought she was going to take out all the garbage cans." Friend Shaun Chang recalled when Ann took out a barrier in a parking garage, then went into the mall and did her shopping.

Once, after visiting Ann at her home, Chris Sullivan started to call a cab to take him back to his hotel, but Ann insisted on driving him herself. "I have to warn you though," Ann said. "I don't make left-hand turns." Sure enough, Ann got Chris back using right turns only. Chris also said that Ann gave one-finger salutes to drivers who honked at her for reasons "unfathomable to her." Matthew Conlon, Cammie King's son, was always amused by Ann's refusal to make left-hand turns. "If she drove, she'd always allow extra time to get to places," said Matt with a chuckle, "because she'd make three right turns for every left."

Everyone I spoke with brought up Ann's generosity. She loved buying in bulk and giving things to people. Most, like me, had flashlight pens. Connie Sutherland said as soon as she picked Ann up at the airport, she'd start pulling little goodies out of her purse. David Simon said Ann started shopping for Christmas gifts in the summer. She never gave him just one Christmas gift; she'd give a shopping bag full. "They'd be small, playful presents like little things to help you open a jar in the kitchen," David remembered. "But no matter how small the gift, she always wrapped it like it came from Tiffany."

Marsha Hunt recalled the day when Ann called and said, "Are you going to be home for the next hour? I'm coming over." An hour later, Ann showed up at Marsha's door bearing a formal evening gown. Ann said, "I bought this dress because it was beautiful, but I don't think that it's becoming on me. When I look at it, it makes me think of you. I think it will probably fit. I hate waste, and it's just wasting away in my closet. If you can use it, fine. If not, give it to someone else."

Author Anne Edwards shared a similar story. One morning, Ann Rutherford arrived at her front door with shoeboxes piled up to her chin. The two had dined together the previous evening. During dinner, Ann saw that her friend's shoes were uncomfortable. So, the next morning she went to her favorite shoe store right when they opened, chose several boxes of shoes for Anne to try on, and carted them to her house. Anne said, "She insisted that I take at least three pairs to wear around the house and see if they'd do."

One day, Anne Edwards, Al, and Ann were going on a trip together. Anne Edwards had recently hurt her leg. Al and Anne Edwards pulled up in front of Ann's house to pick her up. When Al went in to get her, he had to wait while she found just the right cane for Anne Edwards to use. Anne said, "We damn near missed the plane over those canes!" Rose Narva had a similar experience when she hurt her leg, and Ann showed up on her doorstep holding a bundle of canes. "There must have been half a dozen of them," Rose said. "When I asked Ann why she brought so many, she replied, 'You need several to match your outfits.' "

In all my conversations about Ann, her great love for life was a common thread. More than one friend said there was never a time when Ann picked up the phone that she wasn't delighted to hear from you. Jonathan Weedman recalled a party to which he'd escorted Ann and Anne Jeffreys. It was late, and the party was long over, but both women were sitting in the VIP lounge still having a grand old time. "When I said it was time to go," Jonathan said, "they pouted like schoolgirls." Deborah Dozier Potter remembered how much fun Ann was. "When we were kids, Ann would think of games for us to play on long trips in the car," Deborah said. "Ann was incredibly optimistic and positive — very Pollyanna-esque."

Deborah also spoke of Ann's strength. "Did she tell you about her mastectomy?" Deborah asked. I said she hadn't. "She had it in the sixties. Ann was a trailblazer long before Betty Ford. She never complained about it." After the surgery, Ann wore her husband's loose shirts around the house. Her mother, Lucille, asked why she was wearing Bill's baggy shirts when she had so many beautiful blouses. Ann never did tell her mother. She didn't want to upset her. *

"Did Ann tell you about her sister's death?" Deborah asked. Again, I answered no. "Judith took her own life. The story goes that one day she went to Santa Barbara and never returned. It devastated Ann, of course. They were best friends. When Ann was young, her father abandoned the family. Ann's mother was left alone with two young girls and her mother. It makes sense that Ann didn't tell you any of this. She didn't burden anyone with her troubles. She never complained about anything she was going through."

"Did Ann ever make contact with her father?" I asked.

"No. I heard that he appeared at a *Gone With the Wind* event once, but I seem to recall that their meeting was very brief." Deborah paused. "I want to tell you a story. And it's OK to publish this. There's only one polite way to say it. My father was a ladies' man. Everyone knew it, and Ann was well aware of it. It wasn't a secret between the two of them. Ann didn't want to end another marriage. They had an 'understanding' as long as he was discreet. Often when I went somewhere with my father, he'd bring along another woman. For some reason he wanted me to be friends with them. I never liked it, but I couldn't tell him that. And I couldn't tell Ann. We never discussed it.

"After my father died, I flew to L.A. and drove around with Ann to make the necessary arrangements. We went to the funeral home, then over to the church. In the car, I said, 'Ann, there was something

---

* Ann's mastectomy was performed by Marcus Rabwin, a surgeon at Cedars-Sinai Hospital and husband of Marcella Rabwin, who was David Selznick's executive assistant during the filming of *Gone With the Wind*.

I could never tell you, but now I can.' Then I told her how I felt about my father's bringing his dates along all the time. Ann felt badly that he'd put me in those awkward situations.

"When Ann and I arrived at the church, we met with a man who said he needed a list of songs for the organist to play at the funeral. We hadn't thought of that. He needed it right away, so the two of us went out to the car and thought of the songs. Ann picked 'Hurray for Hollywood.' Bill would have liked that. I picked 'Take Me Out to the Ball Game.' He loved baseball. 'How about "I've Got the World on a String"?' I suggested. Ann said that was perfect. But we still needed one more song. Then a huge smile spread across Ann's face. 'I've *got* it!' she said. ' "Thank Heaven for Little Girls!" ' We both almost peed laughing. And — we kept the song *in*. They played it at my father's funeral!"

As the months went by and I continued to write, Ann's house was emptied. Gloria donated Ann's Cadillac to a museum and her clothes to a center that helped women in need. Al was given much of the movie memorabilia. Another friend purchased the *Pride and Prejudice* portrait that hung in the powder room. Most of Ann's antiques, art, and personal effects were auctioned at Abel's Auction House. The week before the auction, I called and asked if there was a stuffed Mickey Mouse in any of the lots. I wanted to bid on it. There wasn't. I discovered one furniture dealer in Hollywood who had purchased much of Ann's furniture. He had been a big fan of Ann's. He said that he'd since sold many of the pieces, but was happy to report that they were now in fine homes where they would be taken care of. I was happy about that, too.

Then one day I received an e-mail from Gloria saying that Ann's house had been sold. It was all gone now. I would never see any of it again. The scattering of her things saddened me, but it also encouraged me to press on with the book. Her things might be gone, but not her memory. I devoted myself to preserving it.

Over the next year, I contacted research libraries, museums, and film festivals. I wrote letters to reporters who had interviewed Ann, fans, neighbors, friends, and fellow actors from the golden age. Unfortunately, there weren't too many of them around anymore. When I asked Chris about Al, he said that after Ann's death Al sold his bungalow and moved himself into an old folks' home. Ann's death had devastated him. As the months went by, I received letters and phone calls from a few of Ann's "sorority sisters" who were still around: Debbie Reynolds, Jane Withers, and Joan Leslie. Mickey Rooney's son wrote on behalf of his father who, now in his nineties, was just too frail to participate. Deborah Dozier Potter wrote that when Ann passed away, her aunt, Olivia de Havilland, phoned her very saddened. Olivia said she'd always loved Ann's optimism, vivacity, and kindheartedness.

But of all of the encouraging notes and letters, none was more special than the one I received a few weeks after Ann passed away. It was a warm Budapest afternoon. I inserted the key into my mailbox and opened it. Inside lay a single pink envelope. I inhaled sharply. This can't be, I thought. Quickly I pulled it out. It was Ann's stationery, and my name was written in Ann's handwriting. But it appeared that someone else had addressed it. The envelope was postmarked after her death. *Could this be from Ann?* I sat down on the steps and felt my heart beating against my chest as I opened it and unfolded the letter. It *was*. The date at the top of the paper revealed that Ann had written the letter a month before I last saw her, about four months before she passed away. But who had mailed it? Perhaps Gloria — or Victor, or Ann's nurse, Marie — had discovered it after Ann's passing and dropped it in the mail. The handwriting was shaky, but the flourish was still there. I held my breath as I read it.

My Dearest Phillip,

You are blessed to work with the word. Keep writing! You mustn't ever give up. Always write about what you love, and always know that I love you. I am including something that I hope will help. And remember my dear — you caused this to happen.

Your Fan Forever,
Ann

Caused this to happen? Caused *what* to happen? *What is she referring to?* I looked inside the envelope, but it was empty. She must not have gotten around to including it. Oh, *what* had she intended to send me?

I read the letter a second time. Beside her name Ann had drawn a heart. That's funny, I thought. She'd never drawn anything on her previous letters. But as I examined the drawing more closely, I realized that it wasn't just a heart. It was her locket! It had the diamond in the center and a few links of the chain. *But why did she take the time to draw her locket?* I leaned my head against the wall and thought about it. And then everything started to come together. Then it all made sense.

Ann sent me her good luck charm. She couldn't send me the real one, so she drew it instead. She'd made me promise to keep writing and now she was passing on her cherished charm to help. But she wasn't just sending me luck. There was another reason. Her locket was a silent witness to her life. Resting all those years against her own heart, it had felt her happiness and her sorrows, the heat of klieg lights and the excitement of premieres. And it knew all her stories — stories from her beloved golden age of Hollywood that she was so proud to have been a part of. "Always write about what you love." I loved Ann Rutherford. And she knew it. In sending me her locket, she was entrusting me with the stories it beheld. *This* is what she wanted to speak with me about for the future. I was sure of it. Just as the wheat carved into the staircase railings had been a sign for her when she moved into her house, this drawing was my sign to write about Ann. As I looked down at the heart, I could hear her voice saying, "Phillip, now let my good luck charm work for you. Protect my stories. Pass them on." I half-laughed, half-cried. Even at the very end of her life, she was living graciously.

I stood up and started to put the letter back into the envelope. Inside it was another piece of paper — a white index card. I hadn't noticed it. I pulled it out, turned it over, and smiled. It was a recipe written by Ann. On the top of the card were five words: *Miss O'Hara's Peanut Butter Soup.*

Miss O'Hara's Peanut Butter Soup

Ingredients:
¼ cup (half a stick) unsalted butter
1 medium onion, finely chopped
2 celery ribs, finely chopped
3 tablespoons flour
8 cups chicken stock
2 cups smooth peanut butter
1¾ cups light cream or half-and-half
Finely chopped salted peanuts

Using medium heat, melt butter in a big pot. Add the onion and celery, stirring until softened. Stir in the flour and cook for a few minutes till it thickens. Pour in chicken stock and bring to a boil. Keep stirring. Lower the heat to medium and cook about fifteen minutes, stirring often. By then it should have reduced and thickened. Through a sieve, pour soup into another pot, making sure to push hard on the solids. Stir the peanut butter and cream into the liquid. Whisking often, warm over low heat for about five minutes. Do not boil. Serve warm with chopped peanuts.

BIBLIOGRAPHY

Bingen, Steven, and Stephen Sylvester and Michael Troyan. *MGM: Hollywood's Greatest Backlot*. California: Santa Monica Press, 2011.

Bridges, Herb. *Gone With the Wind: The Three-Day Premiere in Atlanta*. Georgia: Mercer University Press, 2011.

Cusic, Don. *Gene Autry: His Life and Career*. North Carolina: McFarland & Company Inc., 2010.

Eames, John Douglas. *The MGM Story*. New York: Crown Publishers Inc., 1985.

Edwards, Anne. *Scarlett and Me*. Georgia: The Marietta Gone With the Wind Museum: Scarlett on the Square, 2011.

Fitzgerald, Michael, and Boyd Majors. *Ladies of the Western*. North Carolina: McFarland & Company Inc., 2010.

Flamini, Roland. *Scarlett, Rhett, and a Cast of Thousands: The Filming of Gone With the Wind*. New York: MacMillan Publishing Company, 1978.

Frank, Gerold. *Judy*. Massachusetts: Da Capo Press, 1999.

Myrick, Susan. *White Columns in Hollywood: Reports from the Gone With the Wind Sets*. Georgia: Mercer University Press, 1994.

Paris, James Robert, and Ronald L. Bowers. *The MGM Stock Company: The Golden Era*. New York: Crown Publishers Inc., 1977.

Pratt, William. *Scarlett Fever: The Ultimate Pictorial Treasury of Gone With the Wind.* New York: Macmillan Publishing Company Inc., 1977.

Wagner, Walter. *You Must Remember This.* New York: G.P. Putnam's Sons, 1975.

Wiley Jr., John. *Gone With the Wind: Atlanta's Film, Atlanta's Night.* Georgia: Gone With the Wind Collector's Newsletter, 1990.

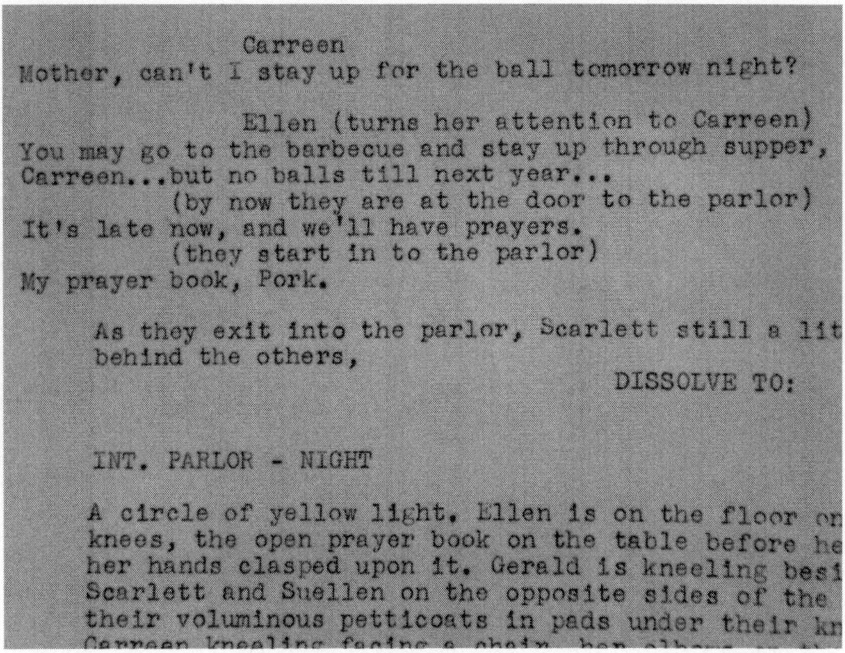

```
                    Carreen
Mother, can't I stay up for the ball tomorrow night?

                    Ellen (turns her attention to Carreen)
You may go to the barbecue and stay up through supper,
Carreen...but no balls till next year...
           (by now they are at the door to the parlor)
It's late now, and we'll have prayers.
           (they start in to the parlor)
My prayer book, Pork.

     As they exit into the parlor, Scarlett still a lit
     behind the others,
                                   DISSOLVE TO:


     INT. PARLOR - NIGHT

     A circle of yellow light. Ellen is on the floor on
     knees, the open prayer book on the table before he
     her hands clasped upon it. Gerald is kneeling besi
     Scarlett and Suellen on the opposite sides of the
     their voluminous petticoats in pads under their kn
     Carreen kneeling facing a chair her elbow
```

A page from Ann Rutherford's *Gone With the Wind* script, including her first line in the picture. The actual lines in the film are different than they appear here. In the film, Carreen says, "Why can't I stay up for the ball tomorrow night? I'm thirteen now." Her mother answers, "You may go to the barbecue and stay up through supper." The line, "but no balls till next year" was omitted. The script does not yet include the part where Suellen tells Scarlett that she doesn't want to wear her "tacky green dress anyway," which prompts Scarlett to pull Suellen's hair.

— image courtesy of Marietta Gone With the Wind Museum.

CONTINUED (2)

Scattered over the field are all that are left of the
people of Tara: The Shot is framed on the Side with the
foreground figure of Gerald (in profile) sitting aimlessly playing with a blade of grass or something of the
sort. The next nearest the CAMERA are Mammy and Prissy;
then a little farther away Suellen and Carreen; and
Scarlett, the farthest away, pulling desperately at a
well rope and swinging the bucket clear of the well brim.
Next to her on the ground are two pails. (Pork is not
in the field as the scene opens, as he is off scene
milking the cow.)

CLOSE SHOT - SUELLEN AND CARREEN

In ragged soiled dresses, they are picking cotton in
sullen silence. Both girls look weary and ill. They
have both only recently gotten over sickness and have
been driven to extremely hard work by Scarlett.

        Suellen (straightening up)
Oh, my back's near broken...
      (with a sob)
Look at my hands!
      (holds them out)
Mother said you could always tell a lady by her hands.

Her hands are scratched and grubby.

        Carreen (sweetly)
I guess things like hands and ladies don't matter so much any
more... You rest, Sue. You're not well yet and I can pick
cotton for both of us.

        Suellen
Scarlett's hateful -- making us work in the fields like --
      (she starts to sob)

        Scarlett's voice
Too bad about that!

Both sisters turn startled and frightened as Scarlett
enters to them. She is carrying two large buckets of
water, which she deposits on the ground.

        Scarlett
Now get back to work! I can't do everything at Tara all by
myself.

        Suellen
What do I care about Tara! I hate Tara!

Another page from Ann Rutherford's original script from *Gone With the
Wind* with Carreen's famous line, "I guess things like hands and ladies
don't matter so much anymore." The lines on this page are exactly as they
appear in the film. The action, however, where Gerald sits aimlessly in
profile and Scarlett pulls at a well rope, do not occur in the picture.
— image courtesy of Marietta Gone With the Wind Museum

ACKNOWLEDGMENTS

As a veteran teacher, I know that when working with children, "it takes a village." The same is true when writing a book. This work would not have been possible without the help of so many people to whom I am sincerely grateful. To the following, I offer my deepest thanks for their support, assistance, and encouragement: Connie Sutherland, Christopher Sullivan, John Wiley Jr., Piotr Konieczka, John Fricke, Debbie Reynolds, James Bawden, Al Morley, Janis Donnaud, Pauline Piekarz, David Hayes, Herb Bridges, Eleanor Bridges, Jason Anderson, Polgarus Studio, Ken Derby, Anne Edwards, Jean Druesedow, Bonnie Strangis, Jane Withers, Betty Graham, Angela Danovi, Kathleen Marcaccio, Jacqueline Gerber, Bill Sasser, William Ruelman, Jonathan Weedman, Mickey Kuhn, Patrick Curtis, Kent State University, Bill Narva, Shaun Chang, Michael Troyan, Steven Bingen, Rose Narva, Anne Jeffreys, Danny Miller, Scott Roberts, Charles Newman, Terry Crane Crabtree, Trent Duffy, Marsha Hunt, Jill Wagner, Linda Lindsley, Sandi Detwiler, Phillip Irwin Cooper, Joan Leslie, Heidi Fisher, Dawn Scheidt, Lennart Guillet, Shauna McGuinnis, Paul Corfield, the Margaret Herrick Library, the Williamsburg Film Festival, Kristine Krueger, Ed Faulkner, Doug Connell, Stephanie Shiro, Diana McInerney, Christine Wait, Bill Russell, Caitlin Hoffman, Peter Ohm, Larry Floyd, Kim Guillet, Guy Kawasaki, Stephen Sylvester, Patrick Picking, Jane Withers, Mary Done, Carol Velazquez, Joan Leslie, Judy Wilson, Knud Jensen, Matthew Conlon, Kevin Zittle for f4 Design, Brian Halley, Deborah Dozier Potter, David Simon, Angela Lansbury, Marilyn Kanes, Olivia de Havilland, and Gloria May — with great appreciation for her assistance and approval to write about her mother.

ANN RUTHERFORD'S FILMOGRAPHY

Student Tour	(uncredited)	1934	MGM
Waterfront Lady	Joan O'Brien	1935	Mascot
Melody Trail	Millicent Thomas	1935	Republic
The Fighting Marines	Frances Schiller	1935	Republic
The Singing Vagabond	Lettie Morgan	1935	Republic
The Lawless Nineties	Janet Carter	1936	Republic
Doughnuts and Society	Joan Dugan	1936	Republic
Comin' Round the Mountain	Dolores Moreno	1936	Republic
The Harvester	Ruth Jameson	1936	Republic
The Oregon Trail	Anne Ridgeley	1936	Republic
The Lonely Trail	Virginia Terry	1936	Republic
Down to the Sea	Helen Pappas	1936	Republic
Annie Laurie (short)	Annie Laurie	1936	MGM
The Devil is Driving	Kittie Wooster	1937	Columbia
Public Cowboy No. 1	Helen Morgan	1937	Republic
Espionage	Train Passenger	1937	MGM
Carnival in Paris (short)	Lisette	1937	MGM
The Bride Wore Red	Third Peasant Girl	1937	MGM
You're Only Young Once	Polly Benedict	1937	MGM
Of Human Hearts	Annie Hawks	1938	MGM
Judge Hardy's Children	Polly Benedict	1938	MGM
Love Finds Andy Hardy	Polly Benedict	1938	MGM
Out West with the Hardys	Polly Benedict	1938	MGM
Dramatic School	Yvonne	1938	MGM
A Christmas Carol	Spirit of Christmas Past	1938	MGM
Four Girls in White	Patricia Page	1939	MGM
The Hardys Ride High	Polly Benedict	1939	MGM
Angel of Mercy (short)	(uncredited)	1939	MGM
Andy Hardy Gets Spring Fever	Polly Benedict	1939	MGM
These Glamour Girls	Mary Rose Wilston	1939	MGM
Dancing Co-Ed	Eve	1939	MGM
Gone With the Wind	Carreen O'Hara	1939	Selznick

Judge Hardy and Son	Polly Benedict	1939	MGM
Andy Hardy's Dilemma (short)	Polly Benedict (uncredited)	1940	MGM
The Ghost Comes Home	Billie Adams	1940	MGM
Andy Hardy Meets Debutante	Polly Benedict	1940	MGM
Pride and Prejudice	Lydia Bennet	1940	MGM
Wyoming	Lucy Kincaid	1940	MGM
Keeping Company	Mary Thomas	1940	MGM
Andy Hardy's Private Secretary	Polly Benedict	1941	MGM
Washington Melodrama	Laurie Claymore	1941	MGM
Whistling in the Dark	Carol Lambert	1941	MGM
Life Begins for Andy Hardy	Polly Benedict	1941	MGM
Badlands of Dakota	Ann Grayson	1941	MGM
This Time for Keeps	Katherine "Kit" White	1942	MGM
The Courtship of Andy Hardy	Polly Benedict	1942	MGM
Orchestra Wives	Connie Ward	1942	Fox
Whistling in Dixie	Carol Lambert	1942	MGM
Happy Land	Lenore Prentiss	1943	Fox
Whistling in Brooklyn	Carol Lambert	1943	MGM
Bermuda Mystery	Constance Martin	1944	Fox
Two O'Clock Courage	Patty Mitchell	1945	RKO
Bedside Manner	Lola Cross	1945	Stone
The Madonna's Secret	Linda	1946	Republic
Murder in the Music Hall	Gracie	1946	Republic
Inside Job	Claire Gray Norton	1946	Universal
The Secret Life of Walter Mitty	Gertrude Griswold	1947	Goldwyn
Adventures of Don Juan	Donna Elena	1948	Warner Bros
Operation Haylift	Clara Masters	1950	Lippert
They Only Kill Their Masters	Gloria	1972	MGM
Won Ton Ton: The Dog Who Saved Hollywood	Grayson's Studio Secretary	1976	Paramount

ANN RUTHERFORD'S TELEVISION CREDITS

Nash Airflyte Theatre	The Doll in the Pink Dress	1950
Stars Over Hollywood	The Kirbys	1951
	Never Laugh at a Lady	1951
Gruen Guild Theater	The Case of the Cavorting Statue	1951
	Unfinished Business	1951
Suspense	Portrait of Constance	1953
Robert Montgomery Presents	Second-Hand Sofa	1953
Willys Theatre Presenting	Cinderella from Cedar Rapids	1953
Ben Hecht's Tales of the City		
General Electric Theater	Woman's World	1953
Lux Video Theatre	Perished Leaves	1954
Climax!	Public Pigeon	1955
	Pale Horse, Pale Rider	1956
Kraft Theatre	Success	1957
Climax!	Four Hours in White	1958
Playhouse 90	The Male Animal	1958
Panic!	Fire Lookout Post	1958
The Red Skelton Hour	Freddie and the Election	1958
Tales of Wells Fargo	The Branding Iron	1959
U.S. Marshal	A Matter of Friendship	1959
The Donna Reed Show	A Difference of Opinion	1959
Perry Mason	The Case of the Howling Dog	1959
	The Case of the Violent Village	1960
	The Case of the Melancholy Marksman	1962
Love, American Style	Love and the Positive Man	1969
	Love and the Impossible Gift	1973
The Bob Newhart Show	My Wife Belongs to Daddy	1973
	An American Family	1974

ABOUT THE AUTHOR

Phillip Done is the author of *32 Third Graders and One Class Bunny: Life Lessons from Teaching* and *Close Encounters of the Third-Grade Kind: Thoughts on Teacherhood*. Currently, Phil lives in Europe, where he teaches at the American International School of Budapest. Visit him at the following sites:

www.anamericaninbudapest.com or www.phillipdone.org.

A portion of the proceeds from *The Charms of Miss O'Hara* will go to the Young Musicians Foundation to help provide instruments for students. Ann would be "happied" by that.

4567540R00174

Printed in Germany
by Amazon Distribution
GmbH, Leipzig